Network Automation with Go

Automate Network Operations and Build Scalable Applications with Go

Tommy Clark

Discover other books in the series

"Go Programming for Beginners: Master Go from Scratch with Easy-to-Follow Steps"

"Web Applications with Go: Unlock the Power of Go for Real-World Web Server Development"

"System Programming with Go: Unlock the Power of System Calls, Networking, and Security with Practical Golang Projects"

"Go Programming for Microservices: Build Scalable, High-Performance Applications with Ease"

"Go Programming for Backend: The Developer's Blueprint for Efficiency and Performance"

"Web Security with Go: Build Safe and Resilient Applications"

"Effective Debugging in Go: Master the Skills Every Go Developer"

Disclaimer

The information provided in *"Network Automation with Go: Automate Network Operations and Build Scalable Applications with Go"* by Tommy Clark is intended solely for educational and informational purposes.

While every effort has been made to ensure the accuracy and completeness of the content, the author and publisher make no guarantees regarding the results that may be achieved by following the instructions or techniques described in this book.

Readers are encouraged to seek appropriate professional guidance for specific issues or challenges they may encounter, particularly in commercial or critical environments.

The author and publisher disclaim all liability for any loss, damage, or inconvenience arising directly or indirectly from the use or misuse of the information contained within this book. Any reliance on the information provided is at the reader's own risk.

Introduction

There has never been a greater need for effective and scalable network operations in the rapidly evolving technology landscape of today. Automation has become essential as businesses try to improve their network infrastructure. This is the intersection of the complex realm of networking with the power of programming. "Network Automation with Go" serves as your entryway to the possibilities of using the flexible Go programming language to automate network operations.

The days of network management being purely a manual process with a lot of human involvement are long gone. Automating time-consuming and repetitive operations is crucial for preserving competitive advantage in a time when agility is crucial and time is money. Go has been a popular option for network automation and application development due to its ease of use, support for concurrency, and strong performance.

This book is intended for software developers, network engineers, and DevOps specialists who want to expand their skill set by implementing automation into their everyday tasks. "Network Automation with Go" offers a thorough and understandable tutorial to using Go for effective network administration, regardless of your level of programming experience.

This book will teach you how to create scalable programs that can easily communicate with a variety of network devices and services, as well as the fundamentals of network automation and Go's special capabilities. We will go over real-world examples, use cases, and best practices to help you with your automation efforts, from automating repetitive operations like monitoring and configuration to creating sophisticated solutions for network diagnostics and administration.

You will learn about the foundational ideas of network automation, how to use Go's capabilities to solve practical networking issues, and the strategies that will put you on the right track as we set out on this exploration together. You will have a firm grasp on how to use automation's efficiency and create robust applications that can expand and change with your network by the end of this book.

Let's begin the process of automating your network operations with Go. Together, we will traverse the fascinating nexus between networking and programming, giving you the skills and information you need to completely transform how you interact and manage your networks. This is "Network Automation with Go." Welcome. Welcome to the networking of the future!

Chapter 1: Introduction to Network Automation with Go

Businesses today demand reliable and secure networks that can adapt to their changing needs. Network automation emerges as a pivotal solution to these challenges, enabling organizations to streamline operations, reduce human error, and enhance overall productivity. In this chapter, we will explore the foundations of network automation, its advantages, and how the Go programming language can serve as an effective tool for implementing these automation solutions.

1.1 Understanding Network Automation

Network automation refers to the use of software to create, manage, and operate network devices and services with minimal human intervention. This shift from manual to automated processes not only saves time but also improves the accuracy of network configuration and management tasks. With the increasing complexity of modern networks, which can span multiple sites and utilize a multitude of devices, automation has become not just practical, but essential.

1.1.1 The Components of Network Automation

Network automation encompasses various components, including:

Configuration Management: Automating the setup and maintenance of hardware and software configurations to ensure consistency and compliance.

Monitoring and Reporting: Continuously observing network performance and generating alerts or reports for potential issues.

Provisioning: Automatically deploying network resources based on pre-defined policies or user requests.

Orchestration: Coordinating multiple automated tasks and workflows to manage complex network changes.

1.1.2 The Benefits of Network Automation

The advantages of adopting network automation are manifold:

Increased Efficiency: Automating routine tasks allows network engineers to focus on strategic initiatives rather than repetitive manual work.

Reduction of Human Errors: Automation reduces the potential for errors that often accompany manual configurations, leading to a more stable and reliable network.

Cost Savings: Efficient use of resources and a reduction in downtime can lead to significant cost savings for organizations.

Scalability: Automated processes are easier to scale, which is critical for organizations that are growing or adjusting to dynamic network demands.

1.2 Why Choose Go for Network Automation?

Go, also known as Golang, is an open-source programming language developed by Google. It has gained tremendous popularity due to its simplicity, efficiency, and strong support for concurrent programming. These characteristics make it particularly suitable for network automation.

1.2.1 Simplicity and Readability

Go's syntax is clean and straightforward, making it accessible for new programmers while still robust enough for experienced developers. This simplicity allows teams to develop, review, and maintain code more effectively, which is crucial in a field where changes and updates are frequent.

1.2.2 Concurrency and Performance

One of the standout features of Go is its built-in support for concurrency, which allows developers to perform multiple tasks simultaneously. This is especially beneficial in network automation, where tasks may involve waiting for responses from multiple devices and systems. Go's goroutines and channels provide a powerful framework to build efficient, high-performance applications.

1.2.3 Strong Standard Library

Go comes with a rich standard library that includes packages for networking, JSON handling, and HTTP servers, among others. This extensive library enables developers to build complex automation tools without relying heavily on external dependencies, fostering a more stable development environment.

1.2.4 Community and Ecosystem

Since its inception, Go has fostered a vibrant community and a plethora of third-party libraries and frameworks. The growing ecosystem of network automation tools and libraries written in Go empowers developers to leverage existing solutions and contribute to new innovations.

1.3 Overview of Network Automation with Go

In the following chapters of this book, we will delve deeper into practical implementations of network automation using Go. We will cover topics such as:

Setting Up Your Go Environment: Ensuring you have the tools you need to start developing automation scripts and applications.

Interacting with Network Devices: Using Go to communicate with devices via protocols such as SSH, SNMP, and REST APIs.

Building Automation Tools: Creating reusable libraries and scripts to automate common network tasks.

Creating a Network Monitoring System: Leveraging Go to build a simple but effective monitoring solution.

Orchestration and Workflow Management: Using Go to coordinate complex network operations across multiple devices.

As the demands on networks continue to evolve, the automation of network management tasks is no longer an option but a requirement. Go's simplicity, performance, and robust ecosystem make it a compelling choice for network automation. Through this book, you will gain practical insights and hands-on experience that will equip you with the skills necessary to implement effective network automation solutions using Go. Let's embark on this journey to transform how networks are managed and operated!

Network Automation with Go Fundamentals

In an era where networks are becoming increasingly complex, the need for automation has never been more important. Network automation involves using software to create, manage, and maintain networks with minimal human intervention. With the rise of DevOps and IT automation, programming languages that are both efficient and powerful have become essential in the toolkits of network engineers.

One such language is Go (or Golang), developed by Google. Known for its simplicity and concurrency features, Go is an excellent choice for network automation tasks. In this chapter, we will explore the fundamentals of network automation using Go, emphasizing key concepts, libraries, and best practices for building scalable and efficient network automation tools.

1. Understanding Go's Strengths

Before diving into network automation, it's important to understand the strengths that make Go a suitable language for this purpose:

1.1 Performance and Concurrency

Go is a statically typed, compiled language that offers excellent performance. The language is designed with concurrency in mind, thanks to goroutines and channels, allowing developers to manage multiple tasks at the same time without the complexity typically seen in multi-threaded programming.

1.2 Simplicity and Readability

Go's syntax is clean and simple, making it easy to learn and read. This attribute reduces the cognitive load on developers, allowing them to focus more on solving problems rather than dealing with a convoluted language structure.

1.3 Strong Standard Library

Go has a rich standard library, including powerful packages for network programming. These libraries facilitate tasks like HTTP requests, TCP/UDP communication, and data serialization, making it easier to interact with network devices.

2. Setting Up Your Go Environment

To get started with network automation using Go, you'll need to set up your development environment. Follow these steps:

2.1 Install Go

Download and install the latest version of Go from the official [Go website](https://golang.org/dl/). Make sure to follow the installation instructions for your specific operating system.

2.2 Configure Your Workspace

After installation, set up your Go workspace. By default, Go uses the `GOPATH` environment variable to determine where to look for packages. You can create a workspace directory at a location of your choice, and within that directory, create folders for your projects.

2.3 Editor Setup

Choose a code editor that you are comfortable with. Popular options for Go development include Visual Studio Code (with the Go extension), GoLand, and Sublime Text. Ensure you have Go tools and formatting enabled for a smoother development experience.

3. Basic Go Syntax for Network Automation

Understanding Go's basic syntax is crucial before building automation scripts. Here is a brief overview of some foundational constructs:

3.1 Variables and Data Types

Go uses static typing, which means variable types are declared during compile time. Here's a quick example:

```go
package main import "fmt"

func main() {

var networkName string = "MyNetwork" var networkID int = 1

fmt.Println("Network Name:", networkName, "ID:", networkID)

}
```

3.2 Functions

Functions are first-class citizens in Go. You can define your functions to encapsulate specific automation tasks.

```go
func pingDevice(ip string) bool {
```

```go
// Logic to ping the device return true // Placeholder
}
```

3.3 Structs

Structs allow you to group data together. For network automation, you can define a struct for network devices:

```go
type NetworkDevice struct { IPAddress string DeviceType string
}
```

4. Network Programming with Go

Now that you've set up your environment and brushed up on Go syntax, we can explore network programming essentials.

4.1 Making HTTP Requests

One of the fundamental tasks in network automation is interacting with APIs of network devices. Go's

`net/http` package allows you to send GET and POST requests easily.

```go
package main

import ( "fmt" "net/http" "io/ioutil"
)

func fetchConfig(ip string) {
```

```go
    resp, err := http.Get("http://" + ip + "/config") if err != nil {

    fmt.Println("Error fetching configuration:", err) return

    }

    defer resp.Body.Close()

    body,        _        := ioutil.ReadAll(resp.Body)
    fmt.Println(string(body))

    }
```

4.2 TCP Connections

For low-level network automation tasks, you might need to establish TCP connections. Go provides the `net` package to facilitate this:

```go
package main

import ( "fmt"

"net"

)

func connectToDevice(ip string, port string) { conn, err := net.Dial("tcp", ip+":"+port)

if err != nil {

fmt.Println("Connection error:", err) return

}

defer conn.Close()
```

```go
fmt.Println("Connected to", ip)
}
```

5. Automation Examples

In this section, we'll examine practical examples illustrating how to automate common network tasks using Go.

5.1 Automating Device Configuration Backup

A common task is to automate the backup of network device configurations. Below is a simple example using HTTP requests:

```go
package main

import ( "fmt"

"os"
)

func backupConfig(devices []NetworkDevice) { for _,
device := range devices {

fmt.Printf("Backing up config for device: %s\n",
device.IPAddress)

// Include logic here to perform the actual backup logic,
e.g., fetching config via HTTP.

}
}
func main() {
```

```go
    devices := []NetworkDevice{
        {IPAddress: "192.168.1.1", DeviceType: "Router"},
        {IPAddress: "192.168.1.2", DeviceType: "Switch"},
    }
    backupConfig(devices)
}
```

5.2 Network Monitoring Script

Another useful automation script could be for monitoring device availability:

```go
package main
import ( "fmt"
"time"
)
func monitorDevices(devices []string) { for {
for _, device := range devices { if pingDevice(device) {
fmt.Printf("Device %s is online\n", device)
} else {
fmt.Printf("Device %s is offline\n", device)
}
}
time.Sleep(10 * time.Second) // Check every 10 seconds
```

19

```
    }
}
```
```

```

We also looked at automation examples that can serve as a foundation for your projects. With Go's performance and capabilities, you're now equipped to tackle automation tasks efficiently in your networking environment.

The Power of Go for Network Automation

In the realm of network automation, the convergence of programming languages, frameworks, and tools has dramatically reshaped the landscape of network management. Among these languages, Go (or Golang) has emerged as a powerhouse, renowned for its efficiency, concurrency, and simplicity. In this chapter, we will explore the unique features of Go that make it particularly well-suited for network automation and delve into practical applications and use cases that illustrate its strengths.

1. Understanding Golang

Go, developed by Google in 2007 and officially released as an open-source language in 2012, is designed for system programming and boasts several features that resonate with network engineers and developers alike. With a succinct syntax and rich standard library, Go emphasizes performance and productivity, making it an excellent choice for writing robust network automation scripts and tools.

1.1 Simplicity and Readability

One of the most significant advantages of Go is its simplicity. The language is designed to be readable and easy to understand, reducing the cognitive load on developers. This straightforwardness means that network engineers, who may not be seasoned programmers, can quickly learn to write scripts, automating routine tasks and enhancing operational efficiency.

1.2 Concurrency

Concurrency is a critical aspect of network operations, where multiple processes often need to run simultaneously—whether for monitoring, data collection, or configuration tasks. Go's built-in support for concurrency through goroutines allows developers to handle numerous network connections concurrently while maintaining excellent performance. This capability is invaluable in scenarios where time-sensitivity is paramount, such as real-time network monitoring or immediate incident response.

1.3 Performance and Efficiency

Go compiles to machine code, delivering performance close to that of C or C++. This feature is particularly important in high-throughput network applications, where processing large volumes of data quickly is essential. Moreover, Go's garbage collection is designed for low-latency environments, minimizing delays during critical operations.

2. Building Blocks for Network Automation

Network automation encompasses various tasks, such as configuration management, monitoring, and data visualization. Go's extensive standard library and community-driven ecosystem provide a wealth of tools and packages that streamline these processes.

2.1 RESTful API Interaction

Many network devices and services expose RESTful APIs for management and monitoring. Using Go's `net/http` package, developers can easily create clients to interact with these APIs, enabling seamless retrieval of statistics, configuration updates, and event handling.

```go
package main

import ( "bytes"
"encoding/json" "net/http"
)

type ConfigUpdate struct { Interface string `json:"interface"` IP string `json:"ip"`
}

func updateConfig(url string, config ConfigUpdate) error {
body, err := json.Marshal(config)

if err != nil { return err
}

req, err := http.NewRequest(http.MethodPut, url, bytes.NewBuffer(body)) req.Header.Set("Content-Type", "application/json")

client := &http.Client{} resp, err := client.Do(req) if err != nil {
```

```go
    return err
}
defer resp.Body.Close()
return nil
}
```

2.2 Network Monitoring

Leveraging Go's concurrency model, developers can create powerful monitoring tools that gather real-time data from multiple devices across the network. The following example demonstrates how to ping a list of devices concurrently to check their availability:

```go
package main

import ( "fmt"
"net"
"sync"
)
func ping(address string, wg *sync.WaitGroup) { defer wg.Done()
_, err := net.Dial("ip4:icmp", address) if err != nil {
fmt.Printf("%s is unreachable\n", address) return
}
fmt.Printf("%s is reachable\n", address)
```

```
}
func main() {

addresses    :=    []string{"192.168.1.1",    "192.168.1.2",
"192.168.1.3"}

var wg sync.WaitGroup

for _, address := range addresses { wg.Add(1)

go ping(address, &wg)

}

wg.Wait()

}
```
```

### 2.3 Configuration Management

Implementing a configuration management tool in Go can
greatly simplify the process of managing network device
configurations. With the use of structured files, such as
YAML or JSON, network engineers can define settings in
a clear, human-readable format. Go can then be used to
parse these files, validate configurations, and apply them
to devices via API or CLI commands.

## 3. The Community and Ecosystem

The growth of Go's community has led to a rich ecosystem
of libraries and frameworks for network automation.
Projects such as **GoNet**, **Gorouter**, and
**goharbor** are examples of tools designed to facilitate
automation and orchestration in network environments.
These projects often bolster collaboration and sharing
among developers, confirming Go's reputation as a first-
```

class language for network automation.

4. Real-World Applications

Numerous organizations have harnessed the power of Go for network automation. For instance, large enterprises use Go to build custom tools that help manage network configurations at scale, handle flow statistics, automate compliance checks, and ensure consistent security policies across their infrastructures.

4.1 Case Study: Automated Configuration Tool

An enterprise-level organization developed an automated configuration tool using Go that interfaces with their supplier's API. They were able to automate the onboarding of new network devices, reducing the time required for deployment from hours to mere minutes. This success not only improved operational efficiency but also minimized human error, leading to more reliable network performance.

The power of Go in the context of network automation cannot be overstated. Offering a combination of simplicity, performance, and concurrency, Go empowers network engineers to craft robust automation solutions that enhance the efficiency and reliability of network operations.

Chapter 2: Go Basics for Network Automation

Among the various languages available, Go (often referred to as Golang) has emerged as a popular choice due to its simplicity, performance, and strong support for concurrent programming. This chapter will introduce you to the basics of Go, focusing on its key features, syntax, and capabilities that make it a suitable option for network automation tasks.

2.1 Why Go for Network Automation?

Before diving into the specifics of Go, it's important to understand why this language is particularly well- suited for network automation:

Concurrency: Network automation often involves communicating with multiple devices simultaneously. Go's built-in concurrency model, with goroutines and channels, makes it easy to handle multiple tasks without the complexity of traditional threading models.

Performance: Go compiles to native code, resulting in fast execution speeds. This is especially beneficial for time-sensitive network tasks, such as responding to events or processing data streams.

Simplicity: The language syntax is clean and straightforward, making it accessible for both beginners and experienced developers. This simplicity facilitates quicker development and easier maintenance of automation scripts.

Robust Standard Library: Go comes with a rich standard library that includes powerful networking packages to simplify the development of network-related applications.

Cross-Platform: Go programs can be compiled for multiple platforms, making it easier to write scripts that can run in different environments without modification.

2.2 Setting Up Go Environment

Before you can start automating network tasks with Go, you need to set up your development environment. Follow these steps:

Install Go: Visit the [official Go website](https://golang.org/dl/) and download the installer for your operating system. Follow the installation instructions to set up Go on your machine.

Set Up Your Workspace:

Go uses a specific workspace structure. By default, your workspace will be in a directory named `go` under your home directory (e.g., `~/go` on Unix-based systems).

Inside the workspace, you'll have three directories: `src` for your source code, `pkg` for compiled packages, and `bin` for executable binaries.

Configure Your Go Path:

You need to set your environment variable `GOPATH` to your workspace path (if you want to use a custom location).

Add the `bin` subdirectory of your workspace to your `PATH` variable to run Go executables globally.

Verify Installation: Open your terminal and run the command:

```bash
go version
```

This should display the installed version of Go, confirming a successful setup.

2.3 Go Language Basics ### 2.3.1 Syntax and Structure

Understanding the basic syntax of Go is crucial for writing network automation scripts. Here's a simple overview:

- **Package Declaration**: Every Go file begins with a package declaration:

```go
package main
```

- **Imports**: Similar to other programming languages, you can include libraries:

```go
import (
"fmt" "net/http"
)
```

- **Main Function**: The entry point of a Go program is the `main` function:

```go
func main() {
```

```go
    fmt.Println("Hello, Network Automation!")
}
```

2.3.2 Variables and Data Types

Go is statically typed, so you need to specify the type of variables. Here are some basic data types:

- **String**:

```go
var message string = "Hello, World!"
```

- **Integer**:

```go
var count int = 5
```

- **Boolean**:

```go
var isActive bool = true
```

You can also use shorthand declaration:

```go
age := 30  // type inferred
```

2.3.3 Functions

Functions in Go are first-class citizens. Here's a function example that adds two integers:

```go
func add(a int, b int) int { return a + b
}
```

2.3.4 Control Structures

Control structures in Go are similar to those in other programming languages. For example, to implement a simple `if-else` statement:

```go
if count > 0 {
fmt.Println("Count is positive")
} else {
fmt.Println("Count is zero or negative")
}
```

2.4 Networking in Go

One of the most compelling features of Go is its powerful networking capabilities. Go makes it easy to perform network operations, from simple HTTP requests to complex socket programming.

2.4.1 Creating a Simple HTTP Server

Creating a basic HTTP server in Go can be done in just a

few lines of code:

```go
package main
import ( "fmt" "net/http"
)
func    helloHandler(w    http.ResponseWriter,    r
*http.Request)  {  fmt.Fprintf(w,  "Hello,  Network
Automation!")
}
func main() {
http.HandleFunc("/",                    helloHandler)
http.ListenAndServe(":8080", nil)
}
```

To run this server, save it in a file named `main.go`, then
execute the following command in your terminal:

```bash
go run main.go
```

Visit `http://localhost:8080` in your web browser, and
you should see the message "Hello, Network Automation!"

2.4.2 Making HTTP Requests

Go's `net/http` package also makes it simple to make
HTTP requests. Below is an example of sending a GET

request:

```go
package main
import ( "fmt"
"log" "net/http"
)
func main() {
response, err := http.Get("http://api.example.com/data")
if err != nil {
log.Fatal(err)
}
defer response.Body.Close()
fmt.Println("Response status:", response.Status)
}
```

This code snippet retrieves data from an API endpoint and prints the response status to the console.

In this chapter, we covered the basics of the Go programming language and highlighted its usefulness in the field of network automation. From setting up your Go environment to understanding the fundamental language features and networking capabilities, you now have a solid foundation to start building network automation scripts. In the following chapters, we will explore more advanced topics and practical applications in network automation using Go, helping you to harness the full potential of this powerful language.

Understanding Go's Syntax

This chapter will delve into the fundamental aspects of Go's syntax, providing a comprehensive overview for anyone seeking to grasp the basics of this powerful language.

1. Basic Structure of a Go Program

A typical Go program consists of packages, imports, functions, and various types of statements. The entry point of a Go application is the `main` package, which contains the `main` function. Here's an example:

```go
package main

import "fmt" func main() {

fmt.Println("Hello, World!")

}
```

1.1 Packages

Go encourages modular programming through the use of packages. Each Go file must specify a package at the beginning. The `main` package signifies that the file is executable and contains the `main` function that's executed when the program runs. Other packages can be imported using the `import` keyword.

1.2 The Import Statement

The import statement allows you to use code from other packages. Go's standard library includes numerous built-in packages, such as `fmt` for formatted I/O and `net/http` for web programming.

1.3 The Main Function

The `main` function is where the execution of a Go program begins. It can take no parameters and does not return a value. The `fmt.Println` function in the example is used to display output in the console.

2. Variables and Types

Go is statically typed, meaning variable types must be declared and are checked at compile time. There are several ways to declare variables:

2.1 Variable Declarations

Variables can be declared using the `var` keyword:

```go
var name string = "Alice"
```

Alternatively, you can use shorthand syntax when declaring and initializing a variable:

```go
age := 30
```

This shorthand can only be used within functions. ### 2.2 Types

Go has several built-in types, including:

Basic Types: `int`, `float64`, `bool`, `string`

Composite Types: `array`, `slice`, `struct`, `map`, `channel` Here's an example of declaring different types of variables:

```go
var (
```

isActive bool = true score int = 100 price   float64 = 99.99

)

```

### 2.3 Constants

Constants are declared using the `const` keyword and must be assigned a value at the time of declaration. They can be of any type.

```go
const Pi = 3.14
```

3. Control Structures

Go has control structures that allow for decision-making and looping: ### 3.1 Conditional Statements

The `if` statement is used for making decisions:

```go
if age >= 18 { fmt.Println("Adult")
} else { fmt.Println("Minor")
}
```
```

3.2 Switch Statement

The `switch` statement is used as an alternative to `if-else` when checking multiple conditions:

```go
switch day { case "Monday":
fmt.Println("Start of the week") case "Friday":
fmt.Println("End of the week") default:


fmt.Println("Midweek")
}
```

3.3 Loops

Go's primary loop structure is the `for` loop, which can be used to iterate over a range, through arrays, or as a traditional loop:

```go
for i := 0; i < 5; i++ { fmt.Println(i)
}
// Looping through a slice
fruits := []string{"Apple", "Banana", "Cherry"} for index, fruit := range fruits {
fmt.Println(index, fruit)
}
```

4. Functions

Functions are first-class citizens in Go. They can be declared with an optional return type and can accept multiple parameters.

4.1 Function Declaration

Here's how to declare and invoke a simple function:

```go
func add(x int, y int) int { return x + y
}

result := add(5, 3) // result now holds the value 8
```

4.2 Variadic Functions

Go supports variadic functions, which can take zero or more parameters of the same type:

```go
func sum(numbers ...int) int { total := 0

for _, number := range numbers { total += number
}

return total
}

result = sum(1, 2, 3, 4) // result holds the value 10
```

5. Error Handling

Error handling is an important aspect of writing robust Go applications. Go uses a simple error handling pattern that returns error values from functions.

```go
func divide(a, b float64) (float64, error) { if b == 0 {

return 0, errors.New("division by zero")

}

return a / b, nil

}
```

Here, the function returns a result and an error. It is the caller's responsibility to check the error before proceeding.

Understanding Go's syntax is essential for writing effective and efficient code. With its clean structure, statically typed nature, and powerful error handling, Go provides a solid foundation for developers. Whether you are building small scripts or large-scale applications, mastering Go's syntax will enable you to leverage the language's full potential.

Key Features of Go for Networking Tasks

Developed by Google, Go has gained significant traction in areas like backend development, cloud computing, and networking due to its performance and ease of use. This chapter delves into the key features of Go that make it particularly suitable for networking tasks, highlighting its strengths in building scalable and robust networked applications.

1. Concurrency Model

One of Go's most touted features is its built-in support for concurrency through goroutines and channels. ### 1.1 Goroutines

A goroutine is a lightweight thread managed by the Go runtime. Instead of spawning threads directly, which can be resource-intensive, developers can create thousands of goroutines to handle multiple network connections concurrently. For instance, a server can manage thousands of clients simultaneously without overwhelming the system:

```go
go func() {
// Handle client connection
}()
```

The efficient management of goroutines allows developers to write non-blocking applications that are able to handle I/O operations, such as reading and writing to network connections, without hindrance.

1.2 Channels

Channels provide a way for goroutines to communicate with each other, allowing for synchronization and data exchange. This becomes particularly useful in networking applications where multiple components must work together seamlessly.

```go
ch := make(chan string)
go func() {
ch <- "Data from goroutine"
}()
data := <-ch fmt.Println(data)
```

Using channels enhances the readability and maintainability of code, ensuring that the flow of information between different parts of a networked application is smooth and organized.

2. Standard Library

Go comes equipped with a rich standard library that simplifies the development of networking applications. The `net` and `net/http` packages provide robust tools for handling TCP and UDP connections, as well as HTTP servers and clients. ### 2.1 Net Package

The `net` package is the cornerstone for networking in Go. It provides functionalities such as establishing connections, creating servers, and managing network protocols. With just a few lines of code, developers can implement a simple TCP server:

```go
ln, err := net.Listen("tcp", ":8080") if err != nil {
log.Fatal(err)
```

```go
}
defer ln.Close()
for {
conn, err := ln.Accept() if err != nil {
log.Println(err) continue
}
go handleConnection(conn)
}
```

2.2 Net/HTTP Package

For web applications, the `net/http` package offers an intuitive interface for building HTTP servers and clients. Developers can create a fully functional web server with minimal setup:

```go
http.HandleFunc("/", func(w http.ResponseWriter, r *http.Request) { fmt.Fprintln(w, "Hello, World!")
})
log.Fatal(http.ListenAndServe(":8080", nil))
```

This ease of use, combined with the power of Go's concurrency model, makes it a prime candidate for modern web services and APIs.

3. Performance

Go boasts impressive performance due to its compiled

nature and efficient garbage collection. Unlike interpreted languages, Go code is compiled into machine code, leading to faster execution. This is especially noticeable in networking applications that require high throughput and low latency.

3.1 Efficient Memory Management

Go's garbage collector is designed to minimize pause times, allowing applications to handle continuous and unpredictable workloads typical in networking scenarios. This ensures that applications remain responsive even under heavy load.

4. Static Typing and Safety

Static typing is one of the elements that sets Go apart from many scripting languages. It allows for type safety during development, reducing the chances of runtime errors related to type conversion and usage. This is critical in networking applications where data integrity and correctness are paramount.

4.1 Strong Typing for Structs

Go allows developers to define custom data structures using structs, which can be used to represent complex data types in network protocols, such as JSON for web APIs or binary data for low-level communication.

```go
type Message struct { ID  int

Body string

}
```

By clearly defining these structures, developers can ensure that network packets are correctly formed and parsed, facilitating smoother communication between systems.

5. Deployment and Cross-Platform Support

Go's build process creates statically linked binaries, making it straightforward to deploy applications without worrying about dependencies or runtime environments. This feature is particularly advantageous for networking applications that need to be deployed across various platforms or in containerized environments like Docker.

5.1 Cross-Compilation

Go makes cross-compilation a breeze, allowing developers to build binaries for different operating systems and architectures with simple flags. This is immensely useful when deploying applications to cloud environments or microservices architectures.

```bash
GOOS=linux GOARCH=amd64 go build -o myapp
```

Go is an exceptional choice for networking tasks, thanks to its concurrency model, rich standard library, performance efficiency, static typing, and ease of deployment. As networked applications continue to grow in complexity and scale, Go's strengths position it well to meet the demands of modern software development. With its combination of powerful features and developer-friendly design, Go is redefining the landscape of networking programming, making it accessible and efficient for developers of all skill levels.

Chapter 3: Getting Started with Go

Known for its simplicity, efficiency, and strong support for concurrent programming, Go has gained popularity among developers for building scalable and high-performance applications. In this chapter, we will explore the fundamental aspects of getting started with Go, including installation, setting up your development environment, and writing your first Go program.

3.1 Installing Go

Before diving into coding, the first step is to install Go on your machine. Go is available for various operating systems, including Windows, macOS, and Linux. Here's how you can install Go on your specific platform.

For Windows

Download the Installer: Visit the [official Go download page](https://golang.org/dl/) and download the Windows installer.

Run the Installer: Double-click the downloaded .msi file and follow the installation instructions.

Set Up the Environment Variables: The installer should handle this automatically, but ensure that the

`GOPATH` and `GOBIN` environment variables are set correctly in your system's Environment Variables. ### For macOS

Use Homebrew: If you have Homebrew installed, you can install Go by running the following command in your terminal:

```bash
```

brew install go
```

**Manual Download**: Alternatively, you can download the macOS package from the [official site](https://golang.org/dl/) and follow the installation instructions.

### For Linux

**Download and Extract**: Open your terminal and use the following commands:

```bash
wget https://dl.google.com/go/go1.20.linux-amd64.tar.gz
sudo tar -C /usr/local -xzf go1.20.linux-amd64.tar.gz
```

(Replace `1.20` with the latest version number.)

Set Up Environment Variables: Add the Go binary to your `PATH`:

```bash
echo "export PATH=\$PATH:/usr/local/go/bin" >> ~/.bashrc source ~/.bashrc
```

Verifying the Installation

To confirm that Go has been installed correctly, open your terminal or command prompt and type:

```bash
go version
```
```

You should see the version of Go that you installed. ## 3.2 Setting Up Your Development Environment

Now that Go is installed, it's important to set up your development environment properly. A good IDE or text editor can boost your productivity. Some popular choices include:

GoLand: A powerful Go IDE by JetBrains, providing intelligent coding assistance and tool support.

Visual Studio Code (VSCode): A lightweight, open-source editor with excellent Go extensions like the official Go extension and Delve for debugging.

Sublime Text: A fast and versatile text editor that you can customize with Go-related plugins. ### Configuring Go Modules

Go modules are essential for managing dependencies in your Go projects. To enable modules, set the `GO111MODULE` environment variable:

```bash
export GO111MODULE=on
```

Creating Your First Project

Let's create a simple Go project to get familiar with the structure and code conventions in Go. Create a new directory for your project:

```bash
mkdir my-first-go-project cd my-first-go-project
```

Initialize a new Go module:

```bash
go mod init my-first-go-project
```

3.3 Writing Your First Go Program

With your project set up, it's time to write your first Go program. Inside your project directory, create a new file called `main.go`:

```go
package main import "fmt"


func main() { fmt.Println("Hello, World!")
}
```

Understanding the Code

Package declaration: Every Go file starts with a package declaration. In this case, `package main` indicates that this file is part of the executable package.

Import statement: The `import "fmt"` statement imports the `fmt` package from the Go standard library, which provides formatting functions.

Main function: The `main` function is the entry point of the program. When the program is executed, this function is called, printing "Hello, World!" to the console.

3.4 Running the Program

To run your Go program, simply execute the following

command in your terminal:

```bash
go run main.go
```

You should see the output:

```
Hello, World!
```

3.5 Building the Executable

Go makes it easy to build your application into a binary executable. To do this, run:

```bash go build
```

This command will generate an executable file in your project directory (named `my-first-go-project` on Linux/Mac or `my-first-go-project.exe` on Windows). You can run it directly by typing:

```bash
./my-first-go-project
``` or
```bash
my-first-go-project.exe
```

In this chapter, we covered the basics of installing Go and setting up your development environment. We wrote a simple program, learned about Go modules, and executed our first binary. As you continue to explore Go, you'll appreciate its robust features and intuitive syntax. In the next chapter, we will dive deeper into the Go language's core concepts, including variables, data types, and control structures, setting the foundation for building more complex applications.

Setting Up Your Go Development Environment

Setting up a Go (Golang) development environment is the first step towards becoming proficient in this powerful programming language. Whether you are a seasoned developer or a beginner, having a well- configured workspace can significantly enhance your productivity and streamline your development workflow. In this chapter, we will guide you through the steps required to set up your Go development environment on various operating systems, configure necessary tools, and establish best practices for managing your Go projects.

1. Installing Go

1.1 Downloading Go

The first step in setting up your Go environment is to install the Go programming language itself. You can download the latest version of Go from the official website:

Go to golang.org/dl

Choose the installer that matches your operating system (Windows, macOS, Linux). Be sure to select the appropriate version based on your system architecture (32-bit or 64-bit).

1.2 Installing Go

Windows:

Run the installer you downloaded.

This will place Go in `C:\Go` by default and add this path to your system's PATH environment variable.

macOS:

You can install Go using Homebrew by running:

```bash
brew install go
```

Alternatively, you can use the downloaded package (`.pkg`) and follow the installation wizard.

Linux:

Extract the downloaded tarball to `/usr/local`:

```bash
tar -C /usr/local -xzf go$VERSION.linux-amd64.tar.gz
```

Append `/usr/local/go/bin` to your PATH variable in `~/.bashrc` or `~/.profile`:

```bash
export PATH=$PATH:/usr/local/go/bin
```

1.3 Verifying the Installation

After installing Go, it's essential to verify that the installation was successful. Open your terminal or command prompt and run:

```bash

go version

```

If installed correctly, this command will display the installed version of Go. ## 2. Setting Up Workspaces

2.1 Understanding Go Modules

Go uses a system called modules for dependency management and project organization. Since Go 1.11, modules have become the standard way to manage Go projects. By creating a Go module, you can easily handle your project's dependencies and avoid conflicts.

2.2 Creating Your First Go Workspace

Choose a directory for your Go projects, for example, `~/go_projects`.

Set the `GOPATH` environment variable to this directory:

- Add the following line to your shell configuration file (`~/.bashrc`, `~/.zshrc`, or equivalent):

```bash

export GOPATH=$HOME/go_projects

```

- Reload the configuration file with:

```bash
```

source ~/.bashrc
```
```

Create a new directory for your Go project within your workspace:

```bash

mkdir     -p     $GOPATH/src/myproject     cd
$GOPATH/src/myproject
```
```

Initialize a new Go module:

```bash

go mod init myproject
```
```

This command creates a `go.mod` file that defines your module and its dependencies. ## 3. Choosing an Integrated Development Environment (IDE)

While you can use any text editor to write Go code, using an IDE or a code editor with Go support can significantly enhance your development experience. Popular choices include:

Visual Studio Code: Highly customizable with excellent Go extensions like the Go extension for auto-completion, debugging, and formatting.

GoLand: A powerful commercial IDE specifically designed for Go programming, offering deep integration with Go's tools.

Atom: A lightweight text editor with Go packages that you can install for syntax highlighting and linting.

Sublime Text: Another lightweight editor with Go-specific plugins. ### 3.1 Installing Extensions for Your IDE

If you choose Visual Studio Code, install the Go Extension:

Open Visual Studio Code.

Go to Extensions (Ctrl+Shift+X).

Search for "Go" and install the official extension by the Go team.

After installation, you may need to install additional tools (like `gopls`, the Go language server) as prompted by the extension.

4. Setting Up Version Control

Using version control is essential for managing changes in your codebase. Git is the most commonly used version control system in Go projects. You can install Git and set up a repository for your project as follows:

4.1 Installing Git

Windows: Git can be installed using an installer from git-scm.com.

macOS: Install Git using Homebrew:

```bash
brew install git
```

Linux: Most distributions come with Git pre-installed, but you can install it using your package manager:

```bash
```

```
sudo apt-get install git
```
```

### 4.2 Initializing a Git Repository Inside your Go project directory, run:

```bash git init git add .
git commit -m "Initial commit"
```

It's good practice to commit your changes frequently. ## 5. Building and Running Go Applications

To build and run your Go application, simply navigate to your project directory and use the following commands:

```bash go build
./myproject  # or .\myproject.exe on Windows
```

Alternatively, you can run your application directly without building an executable:

```bash

go run main.go
```

Having a properly set up Go development environment is crucial for an efficient and pleasant coding experience. By following the steps outlined in this chapter, you should now have Go installed, a workspace configured, an IDE or text editor ready to go, and version control set up. In the coming chapters, we will explore the language features, best practices, and design patterns that make Go a
```

preferred choice for many developers. Happy coding!

Writing Your First Go Program for Network Automation

In this chapter, we will take our first journey into the world of Go programming, specifically targeting applications in network automation. Go, also known as Golang, has gained considerable popularity due to its simplicity, efficiency, and built-in support for concurrency. These features make it an excellent choice for automating network tasks that often require managing multiple devices simultaneously.

Understanding the Basics of Go

Before we begin writing our network automation program, let's briefly review some fundamental concepts of Go:

Installation: To get started, you will need to install Go on your machine. You can download the installer from the [official Go website](https://golang.org/dl/). Follow the installation instructions for your operating system.

Setting Up Your Workspace: After installation, set up your Go workspace. Traditionally, your Go code will reside in a directory structure based on your Go workspace. For simplicity, let's assume you will create a directory named `go-network-automation` in your home directory.

The structure of a Go Program: A basic Go program consists of packages, functions, and imports. The `main` package is special because it is the entry point of the program, while functions contain the logic.

Go Modules: Go modules help you manage dependencies in your Go projects. You can create a new module by running `go mod init <modulename>` in your project directory.

Now, let's go ahead and write a simple program that pings a list of network devices. This program will give us a taste of how to perform basic network automation using Go.

Writing Your First Go Program ### Step 1: Create Your Project

Open a terminal and create a new directory for your project:

```bash
mkdir ~/go-network-automation cd ~/go-network-automation
```

Initialize a new Go module:

```bash
go mod init go-network-automation
```

Step 2: Choose Your Dependencies

To ping devices, we'll use the `os/exec` package, which allows us to run external commands. For more complex network automation tasks, you might later explore libraries like `gopacket` or `go-netconf`.

Step 3: Write the Code

Create a new file named `main.go`:

56

```bash
touch main.go
```

Now open `main.go` in your favorite text editor and add the following code:

```go
package main
import ( "fmt" "os/exec" "strings"
)
func ping(host string) error {
cmd := exec.Command("ping", "-c", "4", host) // for Windows use "ping -n 4 host" output, err := cmd.CombinedOutput()
if err != nil { return err
}
fmt.Printf("Ping results for %s:\n%s\n", host, output)
return nil
}
func main() {
devices := []string{"8.8.8.8", "1.1.1.1", "www.example.com"} // List of IPs or hostnames to ping
for _, device := range devices {
if err := ping(device); err != nil {
fmt.Printf("Failed to ping %s: %v\n", device, err)
}
```

```
}
}
```
```

### Step 4: Explanation of the Code

**Imports**: We import the necessary packages. `fmt` is for formatting output, `os/exec` allows us to run shell commands, and `strings` is used for string manipulation.

**ping Function**: The `ping` function takes a hostname or an IP address as an argument. It constructs a command to execute the `ping` utility, retrieves the output, and prints the results.

**main Function**: In the `main` function, we define a slice of devices (IP addresses and hostnames) we want to ping. We loop through each device and call the `ping` function, handling errors appropriately.

### Step 5: Running the Program

To execute your Go program, return to the terminal and run:

```bash

go run main.go


```

You should see the output of the `ping` command for each device in the list. If successful, you will get the response time and packet loss statistics. If a ping fails, the program will notify you.
```

As you continue your journey into Go and network automation, consider experimenting further with additional network protocols, error handling mechanisms, and even creating APIs for device management. The possibilities are vast, and Go's capabilities will help you automate network tasks more efficiently than ever before.

Chapter 4: Networking (TCP/IP) with Go

Networking is the backbone of modern software applications, enabling communication between servers, clients, and devices across diverse architectures and environments. In this chapter, we will explore how to work with networking protocols, specifically TCP/IP, using the Go programming language. Go's rich standard library and straightforward concurrency model make it an excellent choice for network programming.

4.1 Introduction to TCP/IP

Before diving into the Go code, let's start by revisiting what TCP/IP is. TCP (Transmission Control Protocol) and IP (Internet Protocol) are fundamental protocols in the Internet Protocol Suite. IP is responsible for addressing and routing packets of data between devices, while TCP ensures reliable data transmission.

The layered architecture of TCP/IP includes:

Application Layer: Where applications access the network.

Transport Layer: Managing the delivery of messages across a network, primarily using TCP or UDP.

Internet Layer: Handling packet forwarding, primarily using IP.

Link Layer: Managing the physical connection and data transfer between devices.

Go provides a rich set of libraries for working with these protocols, making it simpler to establish network connections and manage data transfer.

4.2 Setting Up Your Go Environment

Before we start coding, make sure you have Go installed on your machine. You can download it from the official site: golang.org. After installation, you can verify it by running:

```bash
go version
```

You should see the installed version of Go displayed in your terminal. ## 4.3 Building a TCP Server

Let's begin with a simple TCP server. Here, we'll create a server that listens on a specified port and responds with a welcome message to any client that connects.

4.3.1 Writing the TCP Server

Create a new directory for your project and create a file named `tcp_server.go`. Then, add the following code:

```go
package main

import ( "fmt"

"net"

"os"
)

func main() {
// Set up a listener on port 8080
```

```go
listener, err := net.Listen("tcp", ":8080") if err != nil {
fmt.Println("Error starting TCP server:", err) os.Exit(1)
}
defer listener.Close()
fmt.Println("Server is listening on port 8080...")
for {
// Accept new connections conn, err := listener.Accept() if
err != nil {
fmt.Println("Error accepting connection:", err) continue
}
// Handle the connection in a new goroutine go
handleConnection(conn)
}
}
func handleConnection(conn net.Conn) { defer
conn.Close()
fmt.Println("Client                      connected:",
conn.RemoteAddr().String())
// Send welcome message to the client message :=
"Welcome    to    the    TCP    Server!\n"
conn.Write([]byte(message))
}
```
` ` `

4.3.2 Running the Server

To run the server, use the following command in your

terminal:

```bash
go run tcp_server.go
```

You should see the message indicating that the server is listening on port 8080. This server will accept TCP connections and respond with a welcome message.

4.4 Building a TCP Client

Next, let's write a simple TCP client that connects to the server we just created and prints the response it receives.

4.4.1 Writing the TCP Client

Create another file named `tcp_client.go` in the same directory and add the following code:

```go
package main
import ( "bufio" "fmt"
"net"
"os"
)
func main() {
// Connect to the server at localhost:8080 conn, err :=
net.Dial("tcp", "localhost:8080") if err != nil {
fmt.Println("Error connecting to server:", err) os.Exit(1)
}
```

```go
    defer conn.Close()

    // Read the response from the server
    message, err := bufio.NewReader(conn).ReadString('\n') if err != nil {
        fmt.Println("Error reading from server:", err) return
    }

    fmt.Print("Message from server: ", message)
}
```

4.4.2 Running the Client

Open another terminal and run the client with the command:

```bash
go run tcp_client.go
```

You should see a message from the server printed out in the client terminal. ## 4.5 Understanding Error Handling

Error handling is a crucial aspect of building robust network applications. In the examples above, we used basic error checking to ensure that we properly handle potential issues. Consider enhancing error logging and recovery strategies for production-level code, including retries, circuit breakers, and graceful shutdown procedures.

4.6 Concurrency in Go

One of Go's standout features is its goroutines, which

allow concurrent programming with ease. In our server code, each client connection is handled in a new goroutine, allowing multiple clients to connect and receive messages simultaneously. This design is efficient and helps maximize resource utilization.

```go
go handleConnection(conn)
```

This simple line of code enables concurrent handling of connections, which is a significant advantage for network applications.

In this chapter, we introduced the fundamentals of networking with TCP/IP in Go. We created a functional TCP server and client, demonstrating how to accept connections and communicate effectively. As you build more complex applications, you will encounter various networking scenarios and challenges. Understanding the basics of TCP/IP networking with Go will provide a strong foundation for exploring advanced topics such as UDP, HTTP servers, and working with APIs.

Basics of TCP/IP Networking in Go

The Transmission Control Protocol (TCP) and Internet Protocol (IP) are the core protocols of the Internet, forming the backbone of the Internet Protocol Suite, widely known as TCP/IP. This chapter will explore the basics of TCP/IP networking, with a particular focus on how these concepts can be implemented in the Go programming language.

Understanding TCP/IP

TCP/IP is a suite of protocols that governs how data is sent and received over the Internet. It consists of several layers:

Application Layer: This is where user-facing applications operate, utilizing protocols like HTTP, FTP, and SMTP to interact over the internet.

Transport Layer: The transport layer is responsible for providing communication services directly to the application processes running on different hosts. Important protocols include TCP and UDP (User Datagram Protocol).

Internet Layer: This layer handles the routing of data across networks using the Internet Protocol (IP), which is responsible for addressing and packetizing data.

Link Layer: This is the lowest layer, dealing with the physical network hardware and the protocols for communication over the physical medium.

Key Concepts #### IP Addressing

Every device on a TCP/IP network is assigned a unique IP address. This address not only identifies the device but also provides information about its location on the network. There are two versions of IP addresses in use today:

IPv4: A 32-bit address typically represented as four octets (e.g., 192.168.1.1).

IPv6: A more recent version that uses a 128-bit

address and is represented as eight groups of hexadecimal numbers (e.g., 2001:0db8:85a3:0000:0000:8a2e:0370:7334).

TCP and UDP

TCP (Transmission Control Protocol): An orderly and reliable protocol that establishes a connection before data is sent, ensuring that data packets arrive in sequence and without errors.

UDP (User Datagram Protocol): A simpler, connectionless protocol that sends messages without establishing a connection. It is faster than TCP but does not guarantee message delivery or order.

Setting Up a TCP Server in Go

Go's built-in `net` package makes it straightforward to set up a TCP server. Below is a simple example demonstrating a basic TCP server that listens on a specified port and responds to client connections.

```go
package main

import ("fmt"

"net"

"os"

)

func main() {

// Listen for incoming connections on port 8080 ln, err :=
net.Listen("tcp", ":8080")

if err != nil {
```

```go
    fmt.Println("Error starting server:", err) os.Exit(1)
    }
    defer ln.Close()
    fmt.Println("Server is listening on port 8080...")
    for {
    // Accept new connection conn, err := ln.Accept() if err !=
    nil {
    fmt.Println("Error accepting connection:", err) continue
    }
    // Handle the connection in a new goroutine go
    handleConnection(conn)
    }
    }
    // Handle incoming connections
    func handleConnection(conn net.Conn) { defer
    conn.Close()
    fmt.Println("Client connected:", conn.RemoteAddr())
    // Read data from the connection buf := make([]byte,
    1024)
    for {
    n, err := conn.Read(buf) if err != nil {
    fmt.Println("Error reading from connection:", err) return
    }
    fmt.Printf("Received: %s", buf[:n])
```

```go
// Echo the data back to client
_, err = conn.Write(buf[:n]) if err != nil {
fmt.Println("Error writing to connection:", err) return
}
}
}
```

Setting Up a TCP Client in Go

To connect to the server you have just created, you can implement a simple TCP client. Here's how you can do that:

```go
package main
import ( "fmt"
"net"
"os"
)
func main() {
// Connect to the server at localhost on port 8080 conn,
err := net.Dial("tcp", "localhost:8080")
if err != nil {
fmt.Println("Error connecting to server:", err) os.Exit(1)
```

```go
}
defer conn.Close() fmt.Println("Connected to server.")
// Send data to the server msg := "Hello, Server!"
_, err = conn.Write([]byte(msg)) if err != nil {
fmt.Println("Error sending data:", err) return
}
// Read response from the server buf := make([]byte, 1024)
n, err := conn.Read(buf) if err != nil {
fmt.Println("Error reading from connection:", err) return
}

fmt.Printf("Response from server: %s\n", buf[:n])
}
```
```

This chapter covered the essential principles of TCP/IP networking and how to implement a basic TCP server and client using the Go programming language. Understanding these fundamentals is crucial for developing networked applications. As you continue to explore Go's networking capabilities, you'll discover that the language's built-in libraries provide powerful tools for building scalable and efficient network applications.
```

Working with Network Sockets in Go

Go, also known as Golang, offers a simple yet powerful standard library for working with network sockets. This chapter will guide you through the fundamental concepts of network sockets in Go, enabling you to build networked applications effectively.

Introduction to Sockets

At a high level, a socket is one endpoint of a two-way communication link between two programs running on the network. Sockets can be used for various types of communication, including client-server communications. In Go, the `net` package provides the necessary functions and types to work with both TCP and UDP sockets.

Types of Sockets

TCP Sockets

Transmission Control Protocol (TCP) provides a connection-oriented communication channel. TCP ensures reliable data transmission, guaranteeing that data packets are delivered in order and without duplication.

UDP Sockets

User Datagram Protocol (UDP) is a connectionless protocol that allows sending and receiving messages (datagrams). UDP is faster and has less overhead than TCP, but it doesn't guarantee message delivery, order, or error checking.

Setting Up Your Go Environment

Before diving into socket programming, ensure you have a

working Go environment. You can use the Go official website to install it: [golang.org](https://golang.org/dl/).

To create a simple network server, start by creating a new directory for your project:

```bash
mkdir go-socket-example cd go-socket-example
```

Creating a TCP Server

Let's begin by creating a simple TCP server. The server will listen for incoming connections and respond to messages from clients.

Step 1: Import the Required Packages

Start by creating a file named `tcp_server.go` and import the necessary packages:

```go
package main
import ( "bufio" "fmt"
"net"
"os"
)
```

Step 2: Set Up the Listener

Next, create a function to set up a TCP listener:

```go
func main() {
```

```go
// Listen on TCP port 8080
listener, err := net.Listen("tcp", ":8080") if err != nil {
fmt.Println("Error starting TCP server:", err) os.Exit(1)
}
defer listener.Close()
fmt.Println("Server is listening on port 8080") for {
// Accept new connections conn, err := listener.Accept() if err != nil {
fmt.Println("Error accepting connection:", err) continue
}
go handleConnection(conn) // Handle the connection in a new goroutine
}
}
```

Step 3: Handle Incoming Connections

Now, add a function to handle incoming connections:

```go
func handleConnection(conn net.Conn) { defer conn.Close()
fmt.Println("Client connected:", conn.RemoteAddr()) scanner := bufio.NewScanner(conn)
// Read from connection until EOF for scanner.Scan() {
fmt.Println("Received message:", scanner.Text())
```

```go
_, err := conn.Write([]byte("Message received\n")) if err
!= nil {

fmt.Println("Error writing to connection:", err) return

}
}

if err := scanner.Err(); err != nil {

fmt.Println("Error reading from connection:", err)

}

fmt.Println("Client disconnected:", conn.RemoteAddr())

}
```

Step 4: Run the Server

Now you can run your TCP server:

```bash
go run tcp_server.go
```

The server will listen on port 8080 for incoming connections. You should see the message "Server is listening on port 8080".

Creating a TCP Client

Create a simple client to connect to this server. Create a new file named `tcp_client.go` and add the following code:

```go
package main
```

```go
import ( "bufio" "fmt"
"net"
"os"
)
func main() {
// Connect to TCP server
conn, err := net.Dial("tcp", "localhost:8080") if err != nil {
fmt.Println("Error connecting to server:", err) os.Exit(1)
}
defer conn.Close() fmt.Println("Connected to server")
scanner := bufio.NewScanner(os.Stdin)
// Read user input and send to server for {
fmt.Print("Enter message to send (or 'exit' to quit): ")
scanner.Scan()
message := scanner.Text()

if message == "exit" { break
}
_, err := conn.Write([]byte(message + "\n")) if err != nil {
fmt.Println("Error sending message:", err) break
}
// Read response from server
response, err := bufio.NewReader(conn).ReadString('\n')
if err != nil {
```

```go
        fmt.Println("Error reading response:", err) break
    }
    fmt.Print("Server reply: ", response)
    }
}
```

Step 5: Run the Client

Run the client in a separate terminal:

```bash
go run tcp_client.go
```

You can now enter messages to send to the server. The server will respond with "Message received" for each message sent.

Working with UDP Sockets

Now let's look at creating a UDP server and client. The structure is slightly different from TCP. Both the server and client deconstruct data into packets and do not maintain a persistent connection.

Step 1: Creating a UDP Server Create a file named `udp_server.go`:

```go
package main

import ( "fmt"
    "net"
```

```go
    "os"
)
func main() {
// Set up UDP address
addr, err := net.ResolveUDPAddr("udp", ":8080") if err !=
nil {
fmt.Println("Error resolving UDP address:", err) os.Exit(1)
}
// Create a UDP connection
conn, err := net.ListenUDP("udp", addr) if err != nil {
fmt.Println("Error setting up UDP server:", err) os.Exit(1)
}
defer conn.Close()
fmt.Println("UDP server is listening on port 8080") buffer
:= make([]byte, 1024)
for {
n, addr, err := conn.ReadFromUDP(buffer) if err != nil {
fmt.Println("Error reading from UDP:", err) continue
}
fmt.Printf("Received message from %s: %s\n", addr,
string(buffer[:n]))
_, err = conn.WriteToUDP([]byte("Message received\n"),
addr) if err != nil {
fmt.Println("Error sending response:", err)
```

```
}
}
}
```
` ` `

Step 2: Creating a UDP Client Create a file named `udp_client.go`:

```go
package main
import ( "fmt"
"net"
"os"
)
func main() {
// Set up UDP address
serverAddr, err := net.ResolveUDPAddr("udp", "localhost:8080") if err != nil {
fmt.Println("Error resolving server address:", err)
os.Exit(1)
}
```

```go
// Create a UDP connection
conn, err := net.DialUDP("udp", nil, serverAddr) if err !=
nil {
fmt.Println("Error connecting to server:", err) os.Exit(1)
}
defer conn.Close() fmt.Println("Connected to UDP
server")
for {
var message string
fmt.Print("Enter message to send (or 'exit' to quit): ")
fmt.Scanln(&message)
if message == "exit" { break
}
_, err := conn.Write([]byte(message)) if err != nil {
fmt.Println("Error sending message:", err) break
}
buffer := make([]byte, 1024)
n, _, err := conn.ReadFrom(buffer) if err != nil {
fmt.Println("Error reading response:", err) break
}
fmt.Printf("Server reply: %s\n", string(buffer[:n]))
}
}
```
```
```

Step 3: Running the UDP Server and Client First, start your UDP server:

```bash
go run udp_server.go
```

Then, run your UDP client:

```bash
go run udp_client.go
```

As with the TCP client/server, you can send messages, and the server will reply.

In this chapter, you learned the basics of working with network sockets in Go using the `net` package. You created simple TCP and UDP servers and clients, providing a solid foundation for understanding socket programming. With these skills, you can build complex networked systems suited for various applications, ranging from web servers to real-time data processing.

Chapter 5: Core Concepts of Network Automation

This chapter delves into the core concepts of network automation, providing the foundational knowledge necessary for understanding its principles, tools, and best practices.

5.1 Definition and Significance

At its core, network automation refers to the use of software tools and applications to create, manage, and optimize networks with minimal human intervention. This automation can range from basic tasks such as configuration management to complex processes like provisioning, orchestration, and monitoring.

The significance of network automation lies in its ability to mitigate human error, enhance operational efficiency, and reduce operational costs. By automating routine tasks, network engineers can focus on higher-value activities, such as strategic planning and architecture design.

5.2 Key Components of Network Automation ### 5.2.1 Configuration Management

Configuration management ensures that all network devices maintain consistent settings and policies. It involves automatically updating configurations across devices based on desired state configurations. Tools such as Ansible, Puppet, and Chef play a vital role in this context, allowing network teams to manage device configurations proficiently.

5.2.2 Orchestration

While configuration management deals with individual

devices, orchestration combines multiple automated tasks into a streamlined workflow. It involves coordinating the operation of various tools and processes to achieve a defined outcome. Technologies like Kubernetes and OpenStack exemplify orchestration in broader IT environments, whereas network-centric orchestration tools facilitate communication between applications and network services.

5.2.3 Provisioning

Provisioning refers to the process of setting up network resources, such as routers, switches, and firewalls, to be ready for use. Automated provisioning allows for rapid deployment, scaling, and management of these resources, an essential capability in dynamic environments such as cloud and microservices architectures.

Tools like Terraform support infrastructure provisioning by enabling scripting of network resources. ### 5.2.4 Monitoring and Analytics

Effective monitoring is crucial for ensuring the health and performance of a network. Automation extends to monitoring tasks, where systems can continuously observe network status, performance metrics, and traffic patterns. Advanced analytics tools utilize machine learning to detect anomalies and predict future issues, enabling proactive resolution and optimization.

5.3 Benefits of Network Automation ### 5.3.1 Increased Efficiency

By automating repetitive tasks, organizations can significantly boost efficiency, freeing up IT staff to focus on strategic initiatives rather than mundane upkeep. This leads to faster deployment times and quicker responses to network changes.

5.3.2 Enhanced Accuracy and Reliability

Automation minimizes human error, a common issue in manual processes. With standardized configurations and automated checks, networks become more reliable, with fewer outages caused by misconfigurations.

5.3.3 Cost Savings

Reducing the need for manual interventions means that organizations can decrease labor costs associated with network management. Furthermore, by improving network reliability and performance, enterprises can avoid downtime costs and enhance customer satisfaction.

5.3.4 Scalability

As businesses grow, so do their network requirements. Network automation facilitates scalability by allowing organizations to quickly add or modify network resources in response to changing business needs without significant manual effort.

5.4 Challenges in Network Automation

Despite its advantages, network automation presents challenges that organizations must address to reap its full benefits:

5.4.1 Complexity

The complexity of modern networks can make automation difficult to implement. Integrating various tools and ensuring they communicate effectively can be a daunting task.

5.4.2 Security Concerns

Automated processes must be secure to prevent unauthorized access and attacks. Organizations must ensure that their automation tools adhere to best security practices and regulations.

5.4.3 Change Management

Transitioning from a manual to an automated environment requires careful change management and cultural shifts within IT teams. Stakeholders must be trained and data must be handled responsibly.

5.5 Best Practices for Implementing Network Automation ### 5.5.1 Start Small

Organizations should begin their automation journey with small, manageable projects. This allows teams to build expertise and confidence before scaling up.

5.5.2 Use Version Control

Employ version control systems for configuration files and automation scripts. This practice manages changes effectively and ensures that teams can roll back to previous configurations if necessary.

5.5.3 Collaborate Across Teams

Network automation is not limited to network engineers. Collaboration between DevOps, security, and operations teams enhances the effectiveness and acceptance of automation initiatives.

5.5.4 Measure Outcomes

Establish metrics to evaluate the success of automated processes. Analysis of these metrics can provide insights for continuous improvement, ensuring that the automation keeps evolving.

As the demand for faster, more efficient network operations grows, embracing network automation becomes increasingly important. Understanding the core concepts discussed in this chapter is essential for organizations looking to remain competitive in an ever-evolving technological landscape. By leveraging automation effectively, businesses can optimize their network resources and position themselves for future growth and innovation.

Automating Routine Network Tasks

The relentless growth of network complexity has made manual configuration and monitoring of networks increasingly strenuous and error-prone. As businesses expand their infrastructure, ensuring smooth operations across routers, switches, firewalls, and servers becomes imperative. To keep pace with this evolving landscape, IT professionals and network engineers are seeking innovative solutions to automate routine network tasks. Go, a statically typed programming language designed for simplicity and efficiency, has emerged as an excellent choice for building tools that can streamline networking operations. In this chapter, we will explore how Go can be employed to automate routine network tasks, highlighting its strengths through practical examples.

Why Use Go for Network Automation? ### 1. Simplicity and Readability

Go is renowned for its clear syntax and minimalistic design. Code written in Go is easy to read and maintain, making it an ideal choice for network automation scripts where clarity is crucial. This simplicity promotes collaboration among team members and facilitates quicker onboarding for new developers.

2. Concurrency

One of Go's standout features is its built-in support for concurrency through goroutines and channels. Network tasks often involve waiting periods for I/O operations, such as querying network devices or processing configuration files. Go's concurrency model allows developers to run multiple tasks simultaneously, improving the efficiency of network operations and reducing overall execution time.

3. Standard Library and Ecosystem

Go's extensive standard library provides powerful packages for networking, allowing developers to easily handle HTTP requests, manipulate data formats like JSON, and interact with various network protocols. Moreover, the growing ecosystem of third-party libraries and tools extends Go's capabilities, making it suitable for handling low-level network operations as well as high-level automation tasks.

4. Cross-Platform Compatibility

Being a compiled language, Go enables developers to build binaries that run on various operating systems without requiring a separate runtime environment. This cross-platform compatibility is particularly beneficial in heterogeneous network environments where multiple operating systems may be in use.

Setting Up the Development Environment

Before diving into automated network tasks, you need to set up your Go development environment. ### Installation

Download and Install Go: Visit the official Go [downloads page](https://golang.org/dl/) and install the version suitable for your operating system.

Set Up Your Workspace: Create a workspace directory, usually located at `~/go`. This is where you'll store your Go projects.

Configure Your PATH: Ensure that the Go binary directory (`$GOPATH/bin`) is included in your system's PATH to make Go commands easily accessible.

IDE and Extensions

Choose an Integrated Development Environment (IDE) or code editor that supports Go development. Popular options include Visual Studio Code, GoLand, and Sublime Text. Install relevant extensions to enable features such as syntax highlighting, code completion, and debugging.

Automating Basic Network Tasks

Let's explore how we can automate specific network tasks using Go. We will cover three common tasks: pinging hosts, retrieving device information via SNMP, and performing bulk configuration updates on network devices.

Task 1: Pinging Hosts

Pinging is a fundamental networking task, and automating it can help in monitoring the availability of devices. Below is a simple Go program that pings multiple hosts.

```go
package main
import ( "fmt"
"net" "os/exec" "sync"
)
func ping(target string, wg *sync.WaitGroup) { defer wg.Done()
cmd := exec.Command("ping", "-c", "1", target) err := cmd.Run()
if err != nil {
fmt.Printf("%s is unreachable\n", target)
} else {
fmt.Printf("%s is reachable\n", target)
}
}
func main() {
hosts := []string{"8.8.8.8", "8.8.4.4", "1.1.1.1"}
var wg sync.WaitGroup
for _, host := range hosts { wg.Add(1)
go ping(host, &wg)
}
```

```go
wg.Wait()
}
```

This program spawns a goroutine for each host, allowing multiple pings to occur concurrently. The use of

`sync.WaitGroup` ensures that the main program waits for all ping operations to complete. ### Task 2: Retrieving Device Information via SNMP Simple Network Management Protocol (SNMP) is a common protocol used to manage devices on IP networks. The **gosnmp** library makes it easy to perform SNMP queries. Here's an example:

```go
package main

import ("fmt"

"github.com/gosnmp/gosnmp"
)

func main() {
// SNMP Connection
snmpClient      :=      &gosnmp.GoSNMP{      Target:
    "192.168.1.1",

Port: 161,

Version: gosnmp.Version2c, Community: "public",

}
// Connect
err := snmpClient.Connect() if err != nil {
```

```go
    fmt.Printf("Connect() err: %v", err) return
    }
    defer snmpClient.Conn.Close()
    // SNMP Walk to retrieve device information
    oids := []string{".1.3.6.1.2.1.1.1.0", ".1.3.6.1.2.1.1.5.0"}
    for _, oid := range oids {
    result, err := snmpClient.Get([]string{oid}) if err != nil {
    fmt.Printf("Error fetching OID %s: %v\n", oid, err)
    continue
    }
    for _, variable := range result.Variables { fmt.Printf("%s:
    %s\n", variable.Name, variable.Value)
    }
    }
    }
```
```

This example connects to a network device using SNMP, retrieves specified OIDs, and displays the retrieved information.

### Task 3: Bulk Configuration Updates

For larger networks, bulk configuration updates are a routine task. Automating this process can save significant time. Below is a simple implementation that updates device configurations via SSH using the

**golang.org/x/crypto/ssh** package.
```

```go
package main
import ( "fmt"
"golang.org/x/crypto/ssh" "io/ioutil"
"log"
"os"
)
func sshExecute(host string, command string) error {
key, err := ioutil.ReadFile("id_rsa") // path to your SSH
private key if err != nil {
return err
}
signer, err := ssh.ParsePrivateKey(key) if err != nil {
return err
}
config := &ssh.ClientConfig{
User: "username", // replace with your username Auth:
[]ssh.AuthMethod{
ssh.PublicKeys(signer),
},
HostKeyCallback: ssh.InsecureIgnoreHostKey(),
}
client, err := ssh.Dial("tcp", fmt.Sprintf("%s:22", host),
config) if err != nil {
```

```go
return err
}
defer client.Close()
session, err := client.NewSession() if err != nil {
return err
}
defer session.Close()
var output []byte
output, err = session.Output(command) if err != nil {
return err
}
fmt.Printf("Output from %s: %s\n", host, output) return nil
}
func main() {
hosts := []string{"192.168.1.1", "192.168.1.2"}
command := "show running-config" // replace with appropriate command for _, host := range hosts {
err := sshExecute(host, command) if err != nil {
log.Printf("Failed to execute command on %s: %v", host, err)
}
}
}
```

```
```

In this script, the `sshExecute` function connects to a device via SSH and executes a given command, facilitating configuration changes across multiple devices efficiently.

Best Practices for Network Automation with Go

Configuration Management: Use configuration files (e.g., YAML or JSON) to avoid hardcoding sensitive information like usernames and passwords within your scripts. Consider adopting tools like Viper for handling your configuration needs.

Error Handling and Logging: Implement robust error handling to gracefully manage failures. Use logging libraries such as Logrus or Zap to track the execution of tasks and assist in troubleshooting.

Testing and Validation: Before deploying automation scripts in a production environment, ensure thorough testing. Write unit tests to validate functionality and integration tests to reaffirm interactions with real network devices.

Version Control: Maintain your automation scripts in a version control system like Git. This will allow you to track changes, collaborate effectively, and revert to previous versions when necessary.

Documentation: Document your automation scripts clearly, outlining the purpose, usage instructions, and potential caveats. Good documentation fosters understanding and aids in future maintenance.

Automating routine network tasks with Go can significantly enhance operational efficiency, reduce errors, and provide IT teams with valuable insights into their network environments.

Using Go for Automation Workflow Design

The Go programming language, known for its simplicity, concurrency, and performance, stands out as a powerful tool for designing and implementing automation workflows. This chapter delves into the principles and techniques of using Go for automation workflow design, providing you with insights and practical examples to foster your understanding.

1. Understanding Automation Workflows

Before diving into the intricacies of Go, it's essential to grasp what an automation workflow is. An automation workflow is essentially a sequence of tasks that are executed to achieve a specific process or outcome without the need for human intervention. It typically involves the following components:

Triggers: Events that initiate a workflow (e.g., a file upload, a scheduled time, or an API call).

Tasks: Individual actions that are executed, often in a specified order (e.g., data processing, sending notifications, or executing scripts).

Conditions: Decision points that dictate the flow of the workflow based on certain criteria (e.g., if/else statements).

Outputs: The results produced by the workflow, which may serve as inputs for further processes or be delivered as user feedback.

Understanding these elements allows you to design workflows that automate repetitive tasks, enhance efficiency, and reduce errors.

2. Why Go for Automation?

Go, also known as Golang, offers several advantages that make it an ideal choice for workflow automation: ### 2.1 Simplicity

Go's syntax is clean and straightforward, enabling developers to write clear and maintainable code. This simplicity encourages rapid workflow design and iteration.

2.2 Concurrency

One of Go's standout features is its built-in support for concurrency through goroutines and channels. This allows developers to run multiple tasks simultaneously, making it perfect for workflows that require parallel processing.

2.3 Performance

Compiled to machine code, Go delivers high performance, which is particularly advantageous for workflows that handle large datasets or complex computations.

2.4 Rich Libraries

Go has a rich set of libraries and frameworks that can facilitate various tasks such as network communication, file handling, and JSON processing. This ecosystem provides the tools necessary for building robust automation workflows.

3. Designing an Automation Workflow in Go ### 3.1 Workflow Planning

The first step in designing an automation workflow is to outline the tasks, triggers, and conditions. For instance, suppose you want to automate data backup from a local directory to a cloud storage service. The workflow might include:

Trigger: Scheduled backup every day at midnight.

Tasks:

Check for new files in the local directory.

Upload new files to cloud storage.

Send a notification email upon completion.

Conditions: Ensure the cloud storage is reachable before proceeding with the upload. ### 3.2 Implementing the Workflow

Here's an example Go code snippet that demonstrates this workflow. This simplistic version checks for files in a specified directory, uploads them (simulated), and sends a notification.

```go
package main

import ( "fmt" "io/ioutil" "net/smtp" "os"
"time"
)

const (
localDir     = "./backup/"
cloudStorage  = "simulated-cloud-storage" smtpServer
            = "smtp.example.com" smtpPort = "587"
```

```go
    senderEmail =              "your-email@example.com"
    senderPassword = "your-password" recipientEmail =
    "recipient@example.com"
)
func main() { for {

err := backup() if err != nil {

fmt.Printf("Error: %v\n", err)

}

// Wait for 24 hours before the next backup time.Sleep(24
* time.Hour)

}

}

func backup() error {

files, err := ioutil.ReadDir(localDir) if err != nil {

return err

}

for _, file := range files { if !file.IsDir() {

err := uploadToCloud(file.Name()) if err != nil {

return err

}

}

}

return sendNotification()

}
```

```go
func uploadToCloud(fileName string) error {
fmt.Printf("Uploading %s to %s...\n", fileName, cloudStorage)
```

// Simulate upload time.Sleep(2 * time.Second)

```go
fmt.Printf("Successfully uploaded %s to %s\n", fileName, cloudStorage) return nil
}
func sendNotification() error {
auth := smtp.PlainAuth("", senderEmail, senderPassword, smtpServer)
msg := []byte("Subject: Backup Completed\r\n\r\nBackup has been completed successfully.")
err := smtp.SendMail(smtpServer+":"+smtpPort, auth, senderEmail, []string{recipientEmail}, msg) if err != nil {
return err
}
fmt.Println("Notification sent!") return nil
}
```

` ` `

3.3 Error Handling & Recovery

In automation workflows, it's crucial to add robust error handling to manage unexpected issues gracefully. Utilize Go's error handling capabilities to ensure that your application can recover from failures, log errors for further inspection, and provide meaningful feedback.

3.4 Monitoring and Logging

Implement logging to track the execution of your workflow. This information can be invaluable for debugging purposes and improving workflow efficiency. Go's built-in log package is a simple solution to integrate logging into your application.

4. Extending Your Workflow

Once you have a basic workflow in place, you may wish to extend its capabilities. Consider integrating with external APIs for additional functionality, such as fetching data dynamically before executing tasks or notifying different users based on conditions. Additionally, think about using concurrency strategies in Go to improve the execution speed of your workflows.

Using Go for automation workflow design allows developers to create efficient, maintainable, and highly concurrent systems. By understanding the principles outlined in this chapter, you can leverage Go's strengths to automate a wide range of tasks, ultimately leading to improved productivity and reduced manual errors in your operations.

As you explore the capabilities of Go in workflow automation, remember that the landscape is ever-evolving. Continuous learning and adaptation will be your best allies in harnessing the full potential of Go and automation technologies in your projects.

Chapter 6: Configuration Management with Go

Network automation enhances efficiency, reduces human error, and ensures consistency across complex infrastructures. Among the programming languages suited for creating powerful automation scripts, Go—also known as Golang—stands out due to its simplicity, speed, and strong concurrency capabilities. This chapter explores the role of Go in network automation, particularly in configuration management.

6.1 Introduction to Network Automation

Network automation refers to the process of using software to create, manage, and modify networked devices and systems without human intervention. This encompasses various tasks, such as configuration management, monitoring, provisioning, and orchestration of network resources. Automation significantly reduces the likelihood of errors and allows for rapid deployment of configurations across a network.

Understanding the unique challenges posed by networking environments is crucial. Networks can include a mix of hardware and software from various vendors, which often leads to complexities in configuration and management. Tools like Ansible, Puppet, and Chef have been widely used for such tasks, but there's a growing interest in using programming languages like Go owing to its flexibility and efficiency.

6.2 Why Choose Go for Configuration Management?

Go, designed by Google, offers multiple features that make it an ideal choice for network automation: ### 6.2.1

Concurrency and Performance

Go's lightweight goroutines allow for efficient concurrent processing. This is particularly beneficial in network automation, where multiple devices may need to be configured simultaneously. By leveraging concurrency, Go can perform tasks such as querying device status and pushing configurations without blocking operations.

6.2.2 Strong Typing and Simplicity

Go is statically typed, which helps catch errors at compile time, leading to more robust code. Its simplicity allows developers to focus on the logic rather than the complexities often found in other languages. This results in easy maintenance, essential for configuration management systems that require updates and expansions.

6.2.3 Standard Library and Ecosystem

Go has a rich standard library, providing built-in features for networking, JSON handling, and more. Its ecosystem also includes packages for working with REST APIs, making it straightforward to interact with network devices that expose APIs for configuration.

6.2.4 Cross-Compilation

With the ability to compile binaries for different operating systems easily, Go enables deployment across diverse environments. This feature is particularly advantageous in network management, where tools may need to run on various systems, from servers to embedded devices.

6.3 Building a Configuration Management Tool with Go

6.3.1 Setting Up Your Go Environment

Before diving into coding, set up your Go development environment. Visit the official [Go website](https://golang.org/dl/) to download and install the Go toolchain. Once installed, configure your workspace and set your `GOPATH` environment variable.

6.3.2 Creating the Project Structure

A clear project structure is essential for any software project. For our configuration management tool, the following structure will serve as a solid foundation:

```
/network-automation main.go

config/ config.go

devices/ device.go

utils/

utils.go vendor/ go.mod
```

The `main.go` file serves as the entry point, while the other directories hold specific functionalities related to configurations, device interactions, and utility functions.

6.3.3 Implementing Configuration Management
6.3.3.1 Defining Device Models

In the `devices/device.go` file, we define a struct that represents a network device:

```go
package devices
```

```go
type Device struct { Hostname string IP  string
Port    int Protocol string
}
```

6.3.3.2 Managing Configurations

In `config/config.go`, we will create functions to load, validate, and apply configurations:

```go
package config

import ( "encoding/json" "io/ioutil"
)

type Config struct {
Devices []DeviceConfig `json:"devices"`
}

type DeviceConfig struct { Hostname    string `json:"hostname"` IP      string `json:"ip"`
Port    int    `json:"port"`
}

func LoadConfig(filePath string) (Config, error) { var config Config
data, err := ioutil.ReadFile(filePath) if err != nil {
return config, err
}
err = json.Unmarshal(data, &config) return config, err
```

```
}
```

6.3.3.3 Applying Configurations

The next step is to implement a method for applying the configuration to the devices. This could involve using SSH or REST APIs to push configuration changes.

```go
package devices import "fmt"

func ApplyConfiguration(device Device, config string) error {
// Here, implement the logic to interact with the device
// This is a placeholder for the SSH or REST API interaction
fmt.Printf("Applying config to %s at %s:%d\n", device.Hostname, device.IP, device.Port) return nil
}
```

6.3.4 Putting It All Together

In `main.go`, we initiate the application, load configurations, and iterate through each device to apply the respective configurations:

```go
package main

import ( "log"

"network-automation/config"          "network-automation/devices"
```

)

```go
func main() {

cfg, err := config.LoadConfig("path/to/config.json") if err
!= nil {

log.Fatalf("Error loading configuration: %s", err)

}

for _, deviceConfig := range cfg.Devices { device :=
devices.Device{

Hostname: deviceConfig.Hostname, IP: deviceConfig.IP,

Port: deviceConfig.Port, Protocol: "ssh", // For example

}

err := devices.ApplyConfiguration(device, "your-config-
string") if err != nil {

log.Printf("Failed to apply configuration to %s: %s",
device.Hostname, err)

}

}

}
```
```

As the demand for network automation becomes more
pronounced, leveraging programming languages like Go
can simplify and enhance the configuration management
process. In this chapter, we have explored the unique
strengths of Go and how to build a basic configuration
management tool. By leveraging Go's concurrency, ease of
use, and rich libraries, network engineers can streamline
their workflows, reduce errors, and create a more efficient
network management process.
```

Managing Device Configurations with Go

Automating the configuration and management of network devices enhances efficiency, reduces human error, and increases the agility of network operations. One of the powerful tools that has gained popularity in recent years for such automation tasks is the Go programming language, commonly known as Golang.

Go is celebrated for its simplicity, performance, and concurrency capabilities. When applied to network automation, Go offers a robust framework for managing device configurations—enabling networking professionals to streamline their workflows, manage large-scale networks, and maintain compliance with organizational standards. In this chapter, we will explore how to leverage Go for managing device configurations in network environments.

Why Choose Go for Network Automation?

The choice of programming language in network automation can significantly impact the success of automation initiatives. Here are several compelling reasons to choose Go:

Performance: Go is a compiled language that offers high performance similar to C or C++, making it suitable for network-intensive tasks.

Concurrency: Built-in support for concurrent programming using goroutines allows developers to handle multiple network tasks simultaneously, which is essential for managing numerous devices.

Simplicity: Go's syntax and structure are designed to be simple and readable, reducing the learning curve for new developers and enabling faster development cycles.

Strong Standard Library: Go provides a rich set of libraries for networking, making it easier to implement protocols and work with various data formats.

Community and Ecosystem: With a large and active community, Go continues to expand its ecosystem with libraries and tools specifically useful for network automation.

Getting Started with Go for Network Automation

To begin automating network device configurations with Go, you need to set up your development environment. This includes installing Go and ensuring you have a text editor or integrated development environment (IDE) of your choice. Once you have Go installed, you can create a new project directory and initialize it as a Go module:

```sh
mkdir network-automation cd network-automation

go mod init network-automation
```

Libraries for Networking

Handling device configurations typically involves interacting with devices over protocols like SSH, Telnet, or REST APIs. For this, we can leverage several libraries:

SSH: The `golang.org/x/crypto/ssh` package can be

109

used for SSH connections to network devices.

REST: For devices supporting REST APIs, the `net/http` package allows us to send HTTP requests.

YAML/JSON: For configuration data formats commonly used in networking, the `gopkg.in/yaml.v2` and `encoding/json` packages will be helpful.

Fetching Device Configurations

To illustrate how Go can be used for automating device configurations, let's create a simple application that connects to a network device via SSH, fetches its configuration, and displays it.

Here's a basic example:

```go
package main
import (
"golang.org/x/crypto/ssh" "fmt"
"log" "io/ioutil"
)
func main() {
// Device details
device := "192.168.1.1"
username := "admin" password := "password"
// Configure SSH client config := ssh.ClientConfig{
User: username,
Auth: []ssh.AuthMethod{ ssh.Password(password),
```

```go
	},
	HostKeyCallback: ssh.InsecureIgnoreHostKey(),
}
// Connect to the device
conn, err := ssh.Dial("tcp", device+":22", &config) if err != nil {
	log.Fatalf("Failed to dial: %s", err)
}
defer conn.Close()
// Create a new session
session, err := conn.NewSession() if err != nil {
	log.Fatalf("Failed to create session: %s", err)
}
defer session.Close()
// Execute the command to fetch configuration var b []byte
if b, err = session.CombinedOutput("show run"); err != nil {

	log.Fatalf("Failed to run command: %s", err)
}


}
```
```
```

```
// Print the configuration fmt.Println(string(b))
```

In this example, we establish an SSH connection to a network device and execute the command to display the device's running configuration. Note that error handling and security mechanisms should be more robust for production code.

Managing Configurations: Applying and Validating Changes

Once we can fetch configurations, we can extend our application to include functionality for applying changes and validating configurations. The process generally involves:

Creating Configuration Templates: Define templates for device configurations using formats like JSON or YAML to guarantee consistency across devices.

Applying Changes via SSH/REST: Use the methods demonstrated earlier to send configuration changes to the devices.

Validation: Extract current configurations and compare them with the desired state. This is crucial for ensuring the applied settings are correct.

Example of Applying a Configuration

Assuming we have a YAML file containing our desired configuration, we can read it and push it to the device.

```yaml
# config.yaml hostname: NewRouter interface:
- name: GigabitEthernet0/1 description: Uplink to ISP
```

```
ip_address: 192.168.1.2
subnet_mask: 255.255.255.0
```
```
You would parse this file, construct the necessary SSH commands, and apply them to the device using a similar SSH session as shown previously.

## Logging and Monitoring Changes

For any automation tool, logging and monitoring are essential features. Implement proper logging methods to capture actions taken by the automation scripts. You can use Go's built-in logging library or third-party libraries like `logrus` to create detailed logs.

In addition, consider implementing monitoring tools to provide visibility into device states and any changes made. Solutions like Prometheus combined with Grafana can help visualize this data over time.

Network automation using Go provides a powerful and efficient way to manage device configurations. With the right libraries and programming techniques, networking professionals can automate tedious tasks,

ensuring quicker responses to changes and improving overall operational efficiency. As we move further into the era of digital transformation, the potential of Go in facilitating robust, scalable, and efficient network automation will remain significant.
```

Automating Configuration Changes

Network automation addresses these challenges by enabling the automation of configuration changes, enhancing operational consistency, and reducing the potential for human errors. This chapter will delve into how the Go programming language, with its emphasis on performance, simplicity, and built-in concurrency features, serves as an excellent tool for automating network configuration changes.

Understanding Network Automation

Network automation refers to the use of software to create, deploy, and manage network configurations and workflows without requiring manual intervention. This can include tasks such as:

Provisioning Devices: Automatically setting up network devices when they are brought online.

Configuration Management: Ensuring devices maintain consistent configurations across the network.

Monitoring and Reporting: Automatically generating logs and reports regarding network performance and issues.

Compliance Checks: Verifying that network configurations adhere to established policies and standards.

The benefits of network automation are manifold. Increased speed of deployment, improved reliability of configurations, and enhanced operational efficiency allow organizations to manage their networks more effectively.

Why Go for Network Automation?

Go, also known as Golang, is a statically typed, compiled language designed for concurrency, scalability, and simplicity. Here are several reasons why Go is particularly suited for network automation:

Concurrency: Go's goroutines and channels allow developers to handle multiple tasks simultaneously, which is crucial for managing multiple network devices concurrently.

Performance: As a compiled language, Go offers fast execution speeds, making it ideal for high- performance network applications.

Simplicity: Go's minimalist design reduces the complexity associated with many other programming languages, allowing developers to focus on the logic of their automation scripts instead of wrestling with language intricacies.

Great Standard Library: Go's robust standard library provides built-in support for handling web requests and manipulating data, making it naturally suited for network programming.

Community and Support: The growing Go community offers numerous third-party libraries that can streamline network automation tasks.

Setting Up Your Go Environment

Before you can start automating network configurations, you'll need to set up a development environment for Go.

Install Go: Download and install the latest version of

Go from the [official website](https://golang.org/dl/).

Set Up Workspace: Configure your Go workspace by setting the `GOPATH` environment variable. By default, Go places files in a `go` directory under your home directory.

Install Required Libraries: Install relevant Go libraries for network automation. Popular ones include:

gopacket: For packet manipulation and analysis.

netconf: For NETCONF protocols used in network device configuration.

go-ssh: To manage SSH connections to devices. ## Automating Configuration Changes

Let's explore a basic example of how to automate network configuration changes using Go. We'll create a simple program that connects to a network device via SSH and applies a configuration change.

Example: Automating a Router Configuration

In this example, we'll automate a simple change on a Cisco router, updating its hostname.

```go
package main

import ( "fmt"

"golang.org/x/crypto/ssh" "io/ioutil"

"log"

"time"
```

```go
)
func main() {
// Device credentials device := "192.168.1.1"
user := "admin" password := "password"
newHostname := "NewRouter"
// Setting up SSH client configuration config :=
&ssh.ClientConfig{
User: user,
Auth: []ssh.AuthMethod{ ssh.Password(password),
},
HostKeyCallback: ssh.InsecureIgnoreHostKey(), Timeout:
    5 * time.Second,
}
// Connect to the device
conn, err := ssh.Dial("tcp", device+":22", config) if err !=
nil {
log.Fatalf("Failed to dial: %s", err)
}
defer conn.Close()
// Create a new session
session, err := conn.NewSession()
if err != nil {
log.Fatalf("Failed to create session: %s", err)
}
```

```go
defer session.Close()
// Execute the command to change the hostname
command := fmt.Sprintf("configure terminal\nhostname %s\nend\nwrite memory\n", newHostname) output, err := session.CombinedOutput(command)

if err != nil {

log.Fatalf("Failed to execute command: %s", err)

}

fmt.Println(string(output))

fmt.Println("Configuration Change Applied Successfully!")

}
```

Explanation

SSH Client Configuration: We begin by setting up the SSH client configuration with the necessary credentials and settings.

Establishing Connection: Using `ssh.Dial`, we connect to the network device. This step is critical for ensuring secure communication.

Session Creation: We create a new session to run commands on the device.

Execution of Configuration Changes: Commands are injected into the session to change the hostname, write the changes to memory, and confirm successful execution.

Testing and Validation

After implementing the code, it is essential to thoroughly

test and validate the changes made to the network configuration. Make sure to verify:

The new hostname appears correctly on the device.

Other network functionalities remain unaffected.

Log the changes for accountability.

Best Practices in Network Automation

Version Control: Store scripts in a version control system (e.g., Git) to track changes and collaborate with team members.

Error Handling: Implement robust error handling to ensure scripts can recover gracefully from issues.

Logging and Monitoring: Include logging to capture configuration changes and notify teams of significant events or errors.

Idempotency: Aim for idempotent scripts, where running the same script multiple times leads to the same state.

Testing: Test scripts in a staged environment before deploying them to production.

The combination of Go's performance, simplicity, and concurrency capabilities makes it an excellent choice for network automation tasks. As you explore network automation further, consider the broader impacts it can have on your network operations and the potential for integrating more complex workflows and functionalities. Happy coding!

Chapter 7: Building Automation Frameworks with Go

Whether it's for continuous integration, continuous deployment (CI/CD), testing, or infrastructure management, having a robust automation framework can dramatically enhance productivity and reliability. Go, with its concise syntax, excellent concurrency capabilities, and emphasis on simplicity, is increasingly being used to build automation solutions. This chapter will explore the principles of building automation frameworks using Go, highlighting the language's advantages while providing practical examples and best practices.

Understanding Automation Frameworks

Before diving into the implementation details, it's important to define what an automation framework is. Generally, an automation framework provides a structured environment that facilitates the automated execution of tasks or processes. This includes defining a set of protocols, tools, libraries, and configurations that developers can use to streamline various operations from testing software to deploying applications.

Key Components of Automation Frameworks

Modularity: This involves breaking down the tasks into manageable components. Each module should handle a specific responsibility, facilitating easier maintenance and debugging.

Scalability: An effective framework should be able to scale with the requirements of the project. This could mean accommodating more test cases, integrating additional tools, or handling increased load during deployment.

Integrability: The framework should be able to communicate and integrate seamlessly with other tools and services, such as CI/CD platforms, cloud providers, and monitoring tools.

Usability: A good automation framework should prioritize ease of use, offering clear documentation, straightforward setup instructions, and user-friendly interfaces.

Benefits of Using Go for Automation Frameworks

Go has several features that make it particularly suited for building automation frameworks:

Concurrency Support: Go's goroutines and channels allow for easy concurrent programming, making it an ideal choice for automating tasks that can run in parallel, such as simultaneous API calls or handling multiple deployments.

Performance: Go is a compiled language and is known for its high performance and low latency. This is crucial for automation tasks that may need to run quickly and efficiently.

Simplicity: The language's straightforward syntax ensures that developers can write clear and maintainable code, which is essential in a rapidly changing environment.

Strong Standard Library: Go's extensive standard library includes support for HTTP, JSON, file handling, and other necessary functionalities needed for automation, reducing the reliance on third-party libraries.

Cross-Compilation: Go programs can be easily cross-compiled for different operating systems, making it a great fit for teams that work in diverse environments.

Building a Simple Automation Framework

Let's get hands-on and create a simple automation framework using Go. For our example, we'll build a basic framework to automate the deployment of a web application to a cloud provider and perform health checks post-deployment.

Setting Up the Project

First, create a new Go project directory:

```bash
mkdir go-automation-framework cd go-automation-framework

go mod init go-automation-framework
```

Define the Structure

Create a basic structure for our automation framework:

```
go-automation-framework/ main.go

deployment/ deploy.go health_check.go

utils/

logger.go
```

Implementing the Modules

122

1. Logging Utility

First, we create a simple logging utility in `utils/logger.go`:

```go
package utils

import ("fmt"
"log"
"os"
)
var (
LogFile *os.File
)
func InitLogger() { var err error
LogFile, err = os.OpenFile("automation.log",
os.O_CREATE|os.O_WRONLY|os.O_APPEND, 0666) if
err != nil {
log.Fatal(err)
}
log.SetOutput(LogFile)
}
func LogInfo(message string) { log.Println("INFO:",
message)
}
func LogError(message string) { log.Println("ERROR:",
message)
}
```

```
```

2. Deployment Module

Next, implement the deployment logic in `deployment/deploy.go`:

```go
package deployment

import ( "fmt"

"go-automation-framework/utils"
)

func        Deploy(appName        string)        {
utils.LogInfo(fmt.Sprintf("Deploying application: %s",
appName))
// Simulate deployment process
// Here you would add the code to interact with your cloud
provider. utils.LogInfo("Deployment successful")
}
```

3. Health Check Module

Add health check functionality in `deployment/health_check.go`:

```go
package deployment

import ( "fmt"

"go-automation-framework/utils"
)
```

```go
func        HealthCheck(appName        string)        {
utils.LogInfo(fmt.Sprintf("Performing health check on:
%s", appName))
```

// Simulate health check

// Here you would add the code to verify application
health status. utils.LogInfo("Health check passed")

```
}
```
```

### Putting It All Together

Finally, integrate everything in `main.go`:

```go
package main

import (

"go-automation-framework/deployment" "go-automation-framework/utils"

)

func main() { utils.InitLogger()

appName := "MyWebApp" deployment.Deploy(appName)
deployment.HealthCheck(appName)

utils.LogInfo("Automation process completed")

}
```

Running the Automation Framework

To execute your automation framework, run the following
command in your terminal:
```

```bash
go run main.go
```

Upon execution, you will see log statements indicating the progress of your deployment and health checks, which will be saved to `automation.log`.

Best Practices for Automation Frameworks

When building automation frameworks with Go or any other language, consider the following best practices:

Use Configuration Files: Externalize configuration settings using JSON or YAML files to make your framework more adaptable.

Error Handling: Implement robust error handling mechanisms to gracefully manage failures during automation tasks.

Testing: Write tests for your automation code to ensure reliability and avoid regressions as changes occur.

Documentation: Provide clear and comprehensive documentation to facilitate onboarding for new developers or users of the framework.

Version Control: Keep your code organized in version control (e.g., Git), allowing for collaboration and tracking changes over time.

Go's unique features make it an excellent choice for building scalable and efficient automation solutions. Whether you are working on deployment pipelines, automated testing frameworks, or any custom automation needs, embracing Go can lead to better performance and a

126

more streamlined development process. As you expand your automation capabilities, the principles and practices outlined in this chapter will guide you towards creating robust and maintainable frameworks suited to your organization's needs.

Introduction to Automation Frameworks

With the increasing complexity of software applications and the demand for faster delivery cycles, automation has emerged as a crucial component in the software testing process. Automation frameworks serve as the backbone of test automation, providing structured guidelines that facilitate the design, development, and execution of automated tests. This chapter delves into the core concepts of automation frameworks, their significance, and the various types that exist within the software testing landscape.

1.2 The Need for Automation

The evolution of software development practices has brought forth methodologies like Agile and DevOps, emphasizing rapid iteration and continuous integration. As teams strive to meet the expectation of delivering reliable software quickly, manual testing becomes a bottleneck. Manual testing is not only time-consuming but also susceptible to human error. Automation addresses these challenges by enabling repeatable execution of tests, thereby enhancing accuracy and speeding up the testing process.

Automation frameworks provide the tools and structure

needed to implement automated tests efficiently. Without a proper framework, automated scripts can become challenging to maintain and scale, leading to increased costs and effort over time.

1.3 What is an Automation Framework?

An automation framework is a set of guidelines, principles, and best practices that dictate how to perform test automation. It can include the necessary libraries, tools, and development practices to streamline the automation process. A well-structured framework enhances the efficiency and robustness of the test suite, making it easier to manage and extend as the application evolves.

The main components of an automation framework may include:

Test Libraries: These are reusable code components that can be utilized across multiple test cases, providing common functions and methods.

Test Data Management: Proper handling and storage of data used for testing are vital. Frameworks often include strategies for managing test data effectively.

Reporting and Logging: Automated testing shouldn't be a black box. A framework needs to provide detailed reporting and logging mechanisms to track execution results, failures, and system behavior.

Integration Capabilities: To promote seamless integration with CI/CD pipelines and other tools, frameworks should support various plugins and extensions.

1.4 Types of Automation Frameworks

Several types of automation frameworks cater to different testing needs and scenarios. Understanding these types can help teams select the most suitable framework for their context.

1.4.1 Linear Scripting Framework

This framework involves writing test scripts sequentially in a linear fashion. While it is straightforward, it often leads to duplication and maintenance challenges as the number of tests grows.

1.4.2 Modular Testing Framework

In a modular framework, tests are divided into smaller, independent modules that can be reused. This method promotes reusability and better maintenance, as changes made to any individual module propagate through all tests that use it.

1.4.3 Data-Driven Framework

Data-driven frameworks separate test scripts from the test data. This enables testers to execute the same test with multiple sets of data, thereby increasing coverage without duplicating scripts.

1.4.4 Keyword-Driven Framework

In a keyword-driven framework, test action keywords are defined along with their associated data. This approach allows non-technical stakeholders to contribute to test automation by defining what actions need to be performed without writing code.

1.4.5 Behavior-Driven Development (BDD)

BDD frameworks promote collaborative behavior specifications among stakeholders, developers, and testers. Using a language that is easily understood by all parties (e.g., Gherkin), BDD frameworks enhance communication and alignment on test objectives.

1.5 Benefits of Using Automation Frameworks

The adoption of automation frameworks yields numerous benefits, including:

Consistency: Standardizing testing processes ensures consistency across tests and among various team members.

Scalability: Frameworks facilitate easier scaling of test automation efforts as applications grow or change.

Maintainability: Well-structured frameworks improve the maintainability of test scripts, reducing technical debt over time.

Enhanced Collaboration: With clear guidelines and structures in place, teams can work together more effectively, regardless of their individual skill levels.

In the subsequent chapters, we will explore specific frameworks in greater detail, examine best practices for their implementation, and address the challenges associated with adopting automation in various environments. By understanding and leveraging these frameworks, teams can enhance their testing efforts and ultimately deliver better software products faster and more reliably.

Integrating Go into Automation Pipelines

Automation pipelines are designed to streamline processes such as building, testing, and deploying software, all while minimizing human error and enhancing productivity. In this chapter, we will explore how to effectively integrate Go (Golang) into automation pipelines, focusing on its advantages, best practices, and practical examples that will help you leverage Go's strengths in your automation processes.

1. Understanding Go's Advantages in Automation ### 1.1 Performance

Go is known for its impressive performance, thanks to its compiled nature and efficient garbage collection mechanisms. When integrating Go into automation pipelines, tasks that require significant computational resources can be executed faster and more efficiently compared to interpreted languages. This is particularly important in CI/CD pipelines, where build and deployment times are critical.

1.2 Concurrency

One of Go's standout features is its built-in support for concurrency through goroutines and channels. This allows developers to handle multiple tasks simultaneously with ease, making it an ideal choice for automation tasks that need to run in parallel—such as testing multiple modules or conducting concurrent API calls.

1.3 Tooling and Standard Library

Go has a rich standard library that provides a wide array

of tools for handling tasks typically involved in automation pipelines. From HTTP requests to file manipulation, Go's built-in packages can simplify the development process. Additionally, Go's tooling, including `go get`, `go build`, and `go test`, facilitates seamless integration with automation platforms.

1.4 Cross-Platform Compatibility

Go is designed to be cross-platform, which means your automation scripts can run on various operating systems without significant modifications. This versatility is particularly beneficial in CI/CD environments that may involve different operating systems for development and production.

2. Setting Up Your Go Environment

To successfully integrate Go into your automation pipelines, you need to ensure that your development environment is properly configured. Here's how to set it up:

2.1 Installation

Download Go: Visit the official Go website and download the appropriate installer for your operating system.

Install Go: Run the installer and follow the on-screen instructions.

Set Up Environment Variables: Configure your `GOPATH` and add Go's binary directory to your `PATH`.

2.2 Create a Go Project

Create a new Go project for your automation scripts:

```bash
mkdir my-automation-scripts cd my-automation-scripts
go mod init my-automation-scripts
```

2.3 Write Your First Script

Let's say you want to create a simple automation script that sends a GET request to an API and logs the result. Create a file called `api_request.go`:

```go
package main

import ( "fmt" "net/http" "io/ioutil" "log"
)

func main() {

resp, err := http.Get("https://api.example.com/data") if err != nil {

log.Fatal(err)

}

defer resp.Body.Close()


body, err := ioutil.ReadAll(resp.Body) if err != nil {

log.Fatal(err)

}

fmt.Println(string(body))
```

```
}
```
\` \` \`

2.4 Running the Script

You can execute the script using the following command:

\` \` \`bash

go run api_request.go

\` \` \`

3. Integrating Go into CI/CD Tools ### 3.1 GitHub Actions

GitHub Actions is a powerful CI/CD tool that allows developers to automate workflows directly from their GitHub repositories.

Example Workflow

Here's a sample `.github/workflows/go.yml` file that runs Go tests and builds your application upon pushes to the main branch:

\` \` \`yaml name: Go CI

on:

push:

branches: [main] pull_request: branches: [main]

jobs:

build:

runs-on: ubuntu-latest

steps:

uses: actions/checkout@v2

134

name: Set up Go

uses: actions/setup-go@v2 with:

go-version: '1.18'

name: Install dependencies run: go mod tidy

name: Run tests run: go test ./...

name: Build run: go build -v

3.2 Jenkins

Jenkins is another widely-used automation server that can be easily integrated with Go. #### Example Jenkinsfile

```groovy
pipeline {
agent any
stages {
stage('Build') { steps {
script {
sh 'go build -v'
}
}
}
stage('Test') {
```

```
steps {
script {
sh 'go test ./...'
}
}
}
}
}
```
` ` `

4. Automating Tasks with Go

In addition to integration into CI/CD tools, Go can be used to automate various tasks. ### 4.1 Scripted Automation Tasks

Go can be utilized for scripting to automate repetitive tasks such as data processing, file management, or network operations. For instance, a script that cleans up temporary files can look like this:

```go
package main

import ( "os"
"path/filepath"
)

func main() {
filepath.Walk("./temp", func(path string, info os.FileInfo, err error) error { if err != nil {
```

```
return err
}
if info.IsDir(){ return nil
}
return os.Remove(path)
})
}
```
```

### 4.2 API Integration

Interacting with APIs is a common automation task. Go's HTTP client makes it easy to build scripts that connect to external services for data retrieval or submission.

### 4.3 Debugging and Logging

Integrating logging capabilities into your automation scripts will provide valuable insights and help you troubleshoot issues efficiently. Go's `log` package can be employed effectively for this purpose.

Integrating Go into automation pipelines can significantly enhance your development workflow. By leveraging its speed, concurrency features, and powerful standard library, you can create efficient automation scripts that streamline processes, reduce errors, and improve productivity. As your automation needs evolve, Go will continue to provide the robust tools required to adapt and scale, making it a valuable addition to any automation strategy. Whether you're working with CI/CD tools or scripting everyday tasks,
```

Go's versatility and efficiency will empower you to achieve your automation goals.

Chapter 8: Interacting with Network APIs

In this chapter, we will explore how to interact with network APIs using Go, focusing on making HTTP requests, handling responses, and parsing JSON data. By the end of this chapter, you should feel confident using Go to communicate with external services, whether for web scraping, using RESTful APIs, or integrating with third-party services.

8.1 Introduction to Network APIs

Network APIs allow applications to communicate over the internet, enabling them to send and receive data. Most modern network APIs use the HTTP protocol, which is a request-response model. An API client sends HTTP requests to a server, and the server responds with the requested data, typically formatted in JSON or XML.

In this chapter, we will primarily work with JSON data, which is lightweight and easy to use with Go's built- in libraries. We will cover:

Making HTTP requests (GET, POST, etc.)

Handling HTTP responses

Parsing JSON data

Error handling

Practical examples

8.2 Setting Up Your Environment

To begin, ensure you have Go installed on your machine. You can download the latest version from the [official Go website](https://golang.org/dl/). Additionally, you will need an HTTP client library (although Go's standard library has an excellent implementation, it never hurts to know alternatives). For our examples, however, we will stick to the standard `net/http` package.

Create a new Go project folder and initialize a Go module:

```sh
mkdir network-api-example cd network-api-example

go mod init network-api-example
```

8.3 Making HTTP Requests

Go's `net/http` package provides an easy way to make HTTP requests. Below is a simple example of how to make a GET request.

8.3.1 The GET Request

Let's fetch data from a public API. For this example, we will use the JSONPlaceholder API, a free API for testing and prototyping.

Create a new file named `main.go` and add the following code:

```go
package main

import ( "encoding/json" "fmt"
"net/http" "log"
)
func main() {
```

```go
response, err := http.Get("https://jsonplaceholder.typicode.com/posts") if err != nil {

log.Fatalf("Error fetching data: %s", err)

}

defer response.Body.Close()

if response.StatusCode != http.StatusOK {

log.Fatalf("Error: received status code %d", response.StatusCode)

}

var posts []map[string]interface{}

if err := json.NewDecoder(response.Body).Decode(&posts); err != nil { log.Fatalf("Error decoding JSON: %s", err)

}

for _, post := range posts {

fmt.Printf("ID: %d, Title: %s\n", int(post["id"].(float64)), post["title"].(string))

}

}
```

Explanation:

We first make an HTTP GET request to the JSONPlaceholder API.

We check the response status code to ensure it's successful (200 OK).

We decode the JSON response into a slice of maps.

Finally, we print out the IDs and titles of the posts. ### 8.3.2 The POST Request

Next, let's see how to make a POST request. Modify `main.go` to include a function that creates a new post:

```go
func createPost() {
post := map[string]interface{}{ "title": "foo",
"body":  "bar", "userId": 1,
}
postJSON, err := json.Marshal(post) if err != nil {
log.Fatalf("Error creating JSON: %s", err)


response,                     err                    := http.Post("https://jsonplaceholder.typicode.com/posts", "application/json",
bytes.NewBuffer(postJSON))
if err != nil {
log.Fatalf("Error posting data: %s", err)
}
defer response.Body.Close()
if response.StatusCode != http.StatusCreated {
log.Fatalf("Error:   received   status   code   %d", response.StatusCode)
}
```

```go
var createdPost map[string]interface{}

if err := json.NewDecoder(response.Body).Decode(&createdPost);
err != nil { log.Fatalf("Error decoding JSON: %s", err)
}

fmt.Printf("Created Post ID: %d, Title: %s\n",
int(createdPost["id"].(float64)),
createdPost["title"].(string))

}
```
```

### Explanation:

We define a new post using a map and marshal it to JSON.

We send a POST request with the JSON data and ensure the server responds with a 201 Created status.

Finally, we decode the response to see the created post.

You can call `createPost()` within the `main()` function after the GET request to see both requests in action. ## 8.4 Error Handling

Effective error handling is crucial when interacting with APIs. While the examples above include basic error checks, you might want to enhance them by adding more detailed logging, retries on certain failure conditions, and leveraging Go's `errors` package for more granular control.

In this chapter, we've covered the fundamentals of interacting with network APIs in Go. You've learned how to make both GET and POST requests, handle responses, and parse JSON data. Understanding these concepts

143
```

opens the door to a wide array of applications, from integrating with third-party services to building your own microservices.

Working with REST APIs in Go

Go, with its robust standard library and efficient concurrency model, offers a powerful yet straightforward way to interact with REST APIs. This chapter will delve into the essentials of working with REST APIs in Go, covering the core concepts, practical examples, and best practices.

5.1 Understanding REST APIs

REST, which stands for Representational State Transfer, is an architectural style that leverages the principles of stateless communication and resource representation. RESTful APIs allow clients to communicate with servers via standard HTTP methods such as GET, POST, PUT, DELETE, and PATCH.

Key Concepts of REST:

Resources: In REST, the primary concept is that of a resource, which can be any entity like a user, product, or document. Each resource is identified by a unique URL.

HTTP Methods:

GET: Retrieve data from the server.

POST: Create a new resource on the server.

PUT: Update an existing resource entirely.

PATCH: Update a specific part of a resource.

DELETE: Remove a resource from the server.

Statelessness: Each request from the client to the server must contain all the information the server needs to fulfill that request.

JSON Data Format: Most REST APIs communicate using JSON (JavaScript Object Notation), a lightweight format that is easy to read and write.

5.2 Setting Up Your Go Environment

Before diving into coding, ensure you have Go installed on your machine. As of the time of writing, Go 1.20 or higher is recommended. You can download it from the [official Go website](https://golang.org/dl/).

Install Go: Follow the instructions for your operating system to install Go.

Set Up a Workspace: Create a directory for your Go project, and navigate to it.

```bash
mkdir go-rest-api-example cd go-rest-api-example
```

Initialize a Module: Initialize your Go module for dependency management.

```bash
go mod init go-rest-api-example
```

5.3 Making HTTP Requests

Go provides an `net/http` package that simplifies making HTTP requests. Let's start by making a simple GET request to fetch data from a REST API.

Example: Fetching Data from a Public API

In this example, we will use the JSONPlaceholder API, a free online REST API for testing and prototyping.

```go
package main

import ( "encoding/json" "fmt"
"log" "net/http"
)

// Post represents a blog post structure type Post struct {
UserID              int                `json:"userId"` ID int
        `json:"id"`
Title   string `json:"title"` Body           string
`json:"body"`
}

func main() {

response,                      err                      :=
http.Get("https://jsonplaceholder.typicode.com/posts") if
err != nil {

log.Fatalf("Error fetching the data: %v", err)

}

defer response.Body.Close()

if response.StatusCode != http.StatusOK {
```

```go
log.Fatalf("Error: expected status OK; got %s\n",
response.Status)
}
var posts []Post
if err :=
json.NewDecoder(response.Body).Decode(&posts); err !=
nil { log.Fatalf("Error decoding JSON: %v", err)
}
for _, post := range posts {
fmt.Printf("Post ID: %d, Title: %s\n", post.ID, post.Title)
}
}
```
```

### Explanation:

**Struct Definition**: We define a `Post` struct that matches the JSON structure we expect from the API.

**Making the Request**: We make a GET request to the API and check for errors.

**Response Handling**: We ensure the response status is 200 OK, then decode the JSON response body into a slice of `Post`.

**Displaying Results**: Finally, we iterate over the posts and print the ID and title. ## 5.4 Sending Data to REST APIs

In many applications, you will need to send data to a
```

REST API using POST requests. Let's illustrate this with an example where we create a new post.

Example: Creating a Post

```go
package main
import ( "bytes"
"encoding/json" "fmt"
"log" "net/http"
)
// Post represents a blog post structure type Post struct {
UserID int    `json:"userId"`   Title   string `json:"title"`   Body  string `json:"body"`
}
func main() { post := Post{
UserID: 1,
Title: "My New Post",
Body:   "This is the content of my new post.",
}
postData, err := json.Marshal(post) if err != nil {
log.Fatalf("Error marshalling the post data: %v", err)
}
response,                              err                        := http.Post("https://jsonplaceholder.typicode.com/posts", "application/json", bytes.NewBuffer(postData))
```

```go
if err != nil {
log.Fatalf("Error sending the POST request: %v", err)
}

defer response.Body.Close()

var createdPost Post

if err := json.NewDecoder(response.Body).Decode(&createdPost);
err != nil { log.Fatalf("Error decoding JSON response:
%v", err)
}

fmt.Printf("Created Post ID: %d, Title: %s\n",
createdPost.ID, createdPost.Title)
}
```
```

### Explanation:

**Creating a Post**: We create a `Post` instance with sample data.

**Marshalling**: Convert the `Post` struct to JSON format using `json.Marshal`.

**Making the POST Request**: We send the POST request and check for errors.

**Handling the Response**: Decode the response to retrieve the created post's details. ## 5.5 Error Handling

Effective error handling is crucial when working with REST APIs. Always check for errors after making a request and when decoding the response. Consider implementing
```

retries for transient errors or timeouts through the `http.Client` settings.

5.6 Best Practices

Use Context: For better control of requests, especially with timeouts and cancellation, utilize the

`context` package.

Struct Tags: Use appropriate struct tags (e.g., `json:"field_name"`) to ensure JSON marshalling aligns with the API requirements.

Handle Rate Limiting: Be mindful of the API's rate limits—throttle your requests as needed.

Validation and Logging: Validate incoming data, and log important events to help with debugging.

Environment Variables: Avoid hardcoding sensitive information in your code. Use environment variables for API keys and other configurations.

In this chapter, we have explored the fundamentals of working with REST APIs in Go. We learned how to make GET and POST requests, handle JSON data, and implement basic error handling. As you continue to build more sophisticated applications, remember these principles and best practices to leverage the power of Go in your development journey. The ability to interact with RESTful APIs is essential in modern software development, and with Go's simplicity and performance, you can create efficient and robust applications.

Using SNMP and Other Network Protocols in Go

The Simple Network Management Protocol (SNMP) is a vital component in the ecosystem of network management. It allows for the collection and organization of information about managed devices on IP networks, enabling systems administrators to monitor network performance, identify potential problems, and effectively manage devices. In this chapter, we will explore how to implement SNMP and other network protocols in Go, one of the fastest-growing programming languages known for its simplicity, efficiency, and powerful concurrency model.

We'll begin by introducing the basics of SNMP, then dive into Go's networking capabilities, and finally, illustrate how to implement SNMP and other common protocols such as HTTP and MQTT in Go.

Understanding SNMP ### What is SNMP?

SNMP is a protocol used for managing devices on IP networks. It operates using a client-server (or manager-agent) model, where the SNMP manager communicates with the SNMP agents that reside on network devices. SNMP uses a standardized framework for communication, allowing for interoperability between devices from different manufacturers.

SNMP Manager: The system that controls and monitors the SNMP agents.

SNMP Agent: A network device that reports information to the SNMP manager. ### SNMP Architecture

SNMP's architecture consists of several components:

Managed Devices: Devices such as routers, switches, servers, and printers.

Management Information Base (MIB): A database used for managing the entities in a network. It comprises a hierarchical collection of objects.

SNMP Protocol: The protocol that facilitates the communication between the manager and the agent. ### SNMP Versions

There are three main versions of SNMP:

SNMPv1: The original version, offering limited security, primarily through community strings.

SNMPv2c: An enhancement that introduced improved performance and error-handling capabilities. Security remains based on community strings.

SNMPv3: The latest version, which offers enhanced security features, including authentication and encryption.

Setting Up Go Environment for SNMP

Before diving into coding, ensure you have Go installed on your machine. You can download it from the official [Go website](https://golang.org/dl/).

Installing Dependencies

To interact with SNMP in Go, you'll need an SNMP library. One such library is `gosnmp`, which can be installed using:

```bash
go get github.com/gosnmp/gosnmp
```

SNMP Implementation in Go

Now, let's implement a simple SNMP manager in Go that retrieves information from a device. ### Basic SNMP Example

Here's a basic example of how to perform an SNMP GET operation using the `gosnmp` library.

```go
package main

import (
"fmt"
"log"
"time"
"github.com/gosnmp/gosnmp"
)

func main() {
// Create a new SNMP connection gosnmp.Default.Config
= gosnmp.Default

gosnmp.Default.Host = "192.168.1.1" // Replace with the
target device's IP gosnmp.Default.Port = 161
```

```go
gosnmp.Default.Community          =          "public"
gosnmp.Default.Version = gosnmp.Version2c

// Connect to the target device err :=
gosnmp.Default.Connect() if err != nil {

log.Fatalf("Connect() err: %v", err)

}

defer gosnmp.Default.Conn.Close()

// Perform SNMP GET

oids := []string{"1.3.6.1.2.1.1.1.0"} // OID for system
description result, err := gosnmp.Default.Get(oids) // Get
OID value

if err != nil {

log.Fatalf("Get() err: %v", err)

}

// Print result

for _, variable := range result.Variables {

fmt.Printf("Received OID: %s, Value: %s\n", variable.Oid,
variable.Value)

}

// Delay for visibility time.Sleep(2 * time.Second)

}
```
```

### Program Explanation

**Connection Configuration**: Set up the SNMP connection parameters, including the target device's IP

154
```

address, port, community string, and protocol version.

Connecting: Establish a connection to the SNMP agent using `Connect()`.

GET Operation: Fetch the value associated with the specified OID (Object Identifier).

Display Results: Output the retrieved OID and its value to the console. ## Other Network Protocols in Go

In addition to SNMP, Go provides robust libraries for numerous other network protocols. ### HTTP Client Example

Go has a built-in `net/http` package that makes HTTP operations straightforward. Here's a simple example of an HTTP GET request:

```go
package main

import (

"fmt" "io/ioutil" "net/http"
)

func main() {

response, err := http.Get("https://api.github.com") if err != nil {

fmt.Println(err) return

}

defer response.Body.Close()

body, err := ioutil.ReadAll(response.Body) if err != nil {

fmt.Println(err) return
```

```go
}
fmt.Println(string(body))
}
```

MQTT Example

For interacting with MQTT, another popular network protocol commonly used for IoT applications, you can use the `paho.mqtt.golang` package:

```bash
go get github.com/eclipse/paho.mqtt.golang
```

And here's a simple MQTT publisher example:

```go
package main

import (
"fmt"
"os"
mqtt "github.com/eclipse/paho.mqtt.golang"
)

var f mqtt.MessageHandler = func(client mqtt.Client, msg mqtt.Message) { fmt.Printf("TOPIC: %s\nMESSAGE: %s\n", msg.Topic(), msg.Payload())
}
```

```go
func main() {
opts := mqtt.NewClientOptions().AddBroker("tcp://localhost:1883").SetClientID("go_mqtt_client")
opts.SetDefaultPublishHandler(f)
// Connect to MQTT broker client := mqtt.NewClient(opts)
if token := client.Connect(); token.Wait() && token.Error() != nil { fmt.Println(token.Error())
os.Exit(1)

}
```

```

}
// Publish a message
token := client.Publish("topic/test", 0, false, "Hello MQTT from Go!") token.Wait()
// Disconnect client.Disconnect(250)
```

In this chapter, we explored how to use SNMP and other networking protocols in Go. We covered the fundamentals of SNMP, how to set up a Go environment, and provided examples of SNMP, HTTP, and MQTT implementations. Go's powerful standard library and third-party packages make it an excellent choice for network programming, allowing developers to build efficient and scalable applications for managing networked devices and services.

Chapter 9: Leveraging OpenConfig with Go

OpenConfig offers a promising solution, allowing network operators to manage and monitor their systems more seamlessly. In this chapter, we'll explore how to leverage OpenConfig using the Go programming language, equipping you with the tools to build robust network automation solutions.

9.1 Understanding OpenConfig

OpenConfig is an initiative by network operators and vendors to create a common configuration model for network devices, enabling programmability and interoperability. The use of YANG (Yet Another Next Generation) models allows network configurations to be expressed in a structured manner that is vendor-agnostic.

9.1.1 YANG Models

YANG is a data modeling language that helps model configuration and state data for networks. OpenConfig provides a collection of YANG models that describe the fundamental aspects of networking, such as routing, interfaces, and services.

9.1.2 Benefits of OpenConfig

Vendor Interoperability: Use a single data model to interact with devices from different vendors.

Standardization: Simplifies automation and management by providing consistent data structures.

Extensibility: OpenConfig models can be easily extended to incorporate new features.

Incorporating OpenConfig into your network's API integrations provides a strategic advantage in terms of automation and efficiency, and binding it with Go can yield even better results.

9.2 Setting Up Your Go Environment

To begin integrating OpenConfig with Go, ensure you have a proper development environment set up. You'll need Go installed on your machine, as well as necessary dependencies for handling network operations.

9.2.1 Installing Go

If you haven't installed Go, you can download it from the official site:

```bash https://golang.org/dl/
```

After installation, make sure to set up your Go workspace and PATH correctly. ### 9.2.2 Required Libraries

To interact with OpenConfig models, we'll utilize the following Go packages:

`github.com/openconfig/ygot`

`github.com/golang/protobuf/proto`

`gopkg.in/yaml.v2`

Install these packages using the following command:

```bash
go get github.com/openconfig/ygot

go get github.com/golang/protobuf/proto  go get
gopkg.in/yaml.v2
```

9.3 Using OpenConfig Models in Go

Now that your environment is set up, the next step is to leverage the OpenConfig models in your application. ### 9.3.1 Define Your Model

Start by defining an OpenConfig model that you intend to work with. For instance, if you want to configure interfaces, you can begin by creating a YANG file or download one from the OpenConfig repository.

```yang
module openconfig-interfaces {

namespace  "http://openconfig.net/models/interfaces";
prefix "oc-if";

container interfaces { list interface {

key "name"; leaf name {

type string;
}

container config { leaf enabled {

type boolean;
}
}
```

```
}
}
}
```

9.3.2 Generating Go Code from YANG

Utilize the `ygot` tool to generate Go structures from your YANG models. Use the following command:

```bash
go generate ./path/to/YANG/files
```

The above command will generate Go code that matches your YANG model, allowing you to interact with networking configurations seamlessly.

9.3.3 Implementing a Configuration Example

Here's how to use the generated Go code to configure an interface:

```go
package main

import ( "context" "fmt"
"github.com/openconfig/ygot/genutil"
"github.com/openconfig/ygot/ygot"
)
func main() {
// Create an empty interface object ifs :=
```

```go
&oc.Interfaces_Interface{
Name: ygot.String("Ethernet0"),
Config:        &oc.Interfaces_Interface_Config{Enabled:
ygot.Bool(true)},
}
// Convert the structure to JSON/YAML for RPC message
jsonData, err := genutil.ToJSON(ifs)
if err != nil {
fmt.Println("Error converting to JSON:", err) return
}
// Send this data to your network device using gRPC or
REST   API...   fmt.Println("Configuration   data:",
string(jsonData))
}
```
```

### 9.3.4 Handling Responses

Once you've made changes to the device configuration, it's crucial to handle the responses correctly. Typically, OpenConfig will provide you a read-back of the current configuration state. Utilize the same methodologies to decode the responses:

```go
resp, err := sendConfigRequest(jsonData) // Your
RPC/REST call if err != nil {
fmt.Println("Error sending request:", err) return
}
```
```

```go
interfaceState := &oc.Interfaces_Interface{}

if err := genutil.Unmarshal(resp, interfaceState); err != nil { fmt.Println("Error unmarshaling response:", err)

return

}

// Access interface state

fmt.Printf("Interface %s is %v\n", interfaceState.Name, interfaceState.Config.Enabled)
```
```

## 9.4 Best Practices for Using Go with OpenConfig

**Modularize Your Code**: Structure your code into modules that clearly separate configuration, state handling, and utilities.

**Error Handling**: Implement comprehensive error handling to manage device communication issues gracefully.

**Monitor and Log**: Maintain logs of interactions with devices, especially for configuration changes, to track operational status.

**Testing**: Implement unit tests for your application to ensure your models behave as expected.

By following the steps outlined in this chapter, you can develop robust applications to interact with network devices using a clear and consistent data model. As networks evolve, so too must our tools; using standards like OpenConfig in conjunction with modern programming languages such as Go provides the scalability and reliability that today's networks require.
```

Understanding OpenConfig Standards

OpenConfig stands out as a groundbreaking initiative aimed at establishing a vendor-neutral framework for network management protocols. By utilizing data models that streamline configuration and operational management, OpenConfig facilitates a smoother interaction between various network devices and management software. This chapter delves into the fundamentals of OpenConfig standards and illustrates how to leverage them effectively within Go, one of the most popular programming languages for network application development.

1. What is OpenConfig?

OpenConfig is an open-source initiative that focuses on creating common data models for network devices. It seeks to address the complexities involved in managing diverse networking environments characterized by equipment from multiple vendors. At its core, OpenConfig promotes the following principles:

Vendor-Neutrality: OpenConfig is designed to be agnostic to vendors, meaning that it can work with hardware and software from any manufacturer.

Data Models: The initiative uses YANG (Yet Another Next Generation) models to define the configuration and operational state of network devices.

Interoperability: By standardizing the interface through which users interact with network devices, OpenConfig fosters better communication and integration within multi-vendor environments.

165

OpenConfig defines a comprehensive set of models covering a variety of areas, including routing, interface management, and telemetry, among others. Developers who understand these models can build applications that easily interact with devices adhering to these standards.

2. The Role of Go in Network Development

Go, or Golang, developed by Google, has carved out a distinct niche in network programming. Its concurrent processing capabilities, ease of implementation, and robust standard library make it a great choice for developing network-related applications. Go's performance and simplicity lend themselves well to working with protocols such as gRPC and RESTful APIs, which are commonly used alongside OpenConfig to manage network devices.

Benefits of Using Go for OpenConfig

Concurrency: Go's goroutines make it easy to handle multiple network connections simultaneously, which is essential for managing large-scale environments.

Simplicity: The language's succinct syntax enables developers to create and maintain code more efficiently.

Strong Standard Library: Go's extensive libraries facilitate easy integration with various network protocols, simplifying the implementation of OpenConfig standards.

3. OpenConfig Data Models

3.1 Overview of YANG Models

OpenConfig leverages YANG, a powerful data modeling language, to define its data structures. These models are essential for generating configuration commands and understanding the operational states of devices:

Schema: YAML files define the structure of a configuration or operational state.

Data Types: YANG helps specify various data types like integers, strings, and other complex data structures.

3.2 Examples of OpenConfig Data Models Commonly used OpenConfig models include:

OpenConfig Interfaces: This model enables the configuration and monitoring of network interfaces.

OpenConfig Routing: Useful in defining routing protocols and managing routing tables.

OpenConfig Telemetry: This model manages telemetry data for real-time monitoring and analytics.

3.3 Generating Go Code from YANG Models

To work with OpenConfig models in Go, developers can generate Go structs using tools like `yang-go`. This tool reads YANG model files and produces Go code that adheres to the defined schema.

Example Workflow

Define YANG Model: Create or source a YANG model that fits your requirements.

Generate Go Structs: Use the yang-go tool to generate Go files based on your YANG models.

```
yang-go -output-dir=gen models/*.yang
```

Integrate into Application: The generated structs can now be directly used in your Go application. ## 4. Implementing OpenConfig in Go Applications

4.1 Setting Up a Go Project

To implement OpenConfig in a Go application, follow these steps:

```bash
mkdir openconfig-go-app cd openconfig-go-app

go mod init openconfig-go-app
```

4.2 Creating a Client

Using Go's `net/http` package, you can create an API client to interact with a network device that supports OpenConfig.

```go
package main

import ( "bytes"

"encoding/json" "fmt"

"net/http"
)


type Interface struct {

Name string `json:"name"` Enabled             bool `json:"enabled"`

Description string `json:"description,omitempty"`
```

```go
}
func main() {

newInterface := Interface{ Name: "eth0", Enabled:
    true,

Description: "Primary interface",

}

jsonData, _ := json.Marshal(newInterface)

req, err := http.NewRequest("POST", "http://device-ip:port/openconfig/interfaces",
bytes.NewBuffer(jsonData))

if err != nil { fmt.Println(err)

}

req.Header.Set("Content-Type", "application/json")

client := &http.Client{} resp, err := client.Do(req) if err !=
nil {

fmt.Println(err)

}

defer resp.Body.Close()

fmt.Println("Response status:", resp.Status)

}
```
```

### 4.3 Interacting with Network Devices

Once you have established your client, you can read or modify the configurations according to the OpenConfig standards defined by your YANG models.
```

5. Best Practices

5.1 Keep Security in Mind

When dealing with network management, ensure that you incorporate security best practices such as:

Use HTTPS: Always interact with devices using secure protocols.

Authentication: Implement token-based authentication to secure your API endpoints. ### 5.2 Version Control

OpenConfig models are regularly updated. Regularly check for updates to the YANG models you depend on and make sure to adjust your Go code accordingly.

5.3 Testing

Consider using libraries for mock testing, especially for the client-side logic, to ensure that your interactions with OpenConfig-based APIs work as expected without needing to connect to live devices.

OpenConfig provides a robust framework for managing network devices in a standardized manner, and the Go programming language serves as an excellent tool for implementing these standards. By understanding the principles behind OpenConfig, its data models, and the ways to integrate them within a Go application, developers can create efficient, scalable, and vendor-agnostic network management solutions. As the world of networking continues to develop, familiarity with OpenConfig and Go will become increasingly valuable.

Implementing OpenConfig with Go

The use of OpenConfig is crucial for modern network operators who are seeking automation and consistency in their network management practices. In this chapter, we will explore how to implement OpenConfig using the Go programming language, providing a practical approach to interacting with network devices.

Prerequisites

Before we begin, it is essential to have a basic understanding of:

Go Programming Language: Familiarity with Go syntax, data structures, and creating packages.

OpenConfig Models: An understanding of the OpenConfig data models and their purpose.

gNMI Protocol: Grpc Network Management Interface (gNMI) is a protocol defined by OpenConfig that is used for managing and observing the state of network devices.

For the purposes of this chapter, ensure that you have Go installed on your machine (version 1.14 or higher recommended) and that your workspace is properly set up.

Setting Up the Environment

To implement OpenConfig in Go, we will start by setting up our development environment. Below is a step-by-step procedure for setting up:

Create a new Go module:

```bash
```

```
go mod init openconfig-demo
```
```

**Install necessary dependencies**:

You will need the `gRPC` and `OpenConfig` libraries. Use the following commands:

```bash
go get google.golang.org/grpc
go get github.com/openconfig/gnmi/proto/gnmi
```

Set up the directory structure:

Organizing your project is crucial. The following structure is recommended:

```

openconfig-demo/ main.go

client/

client.go models/

models.go
```

Understanding OpenConfig Models

OpenConfig data models are defined using YANG, which is a data modeling language used to model configuration and operational data. In this section, we will focus on defining a simple model to interact with a network device.

Defining Models

Create a simple YANG model:
```

In a file named `simple.yang` under the `models` directory, define a basic model for interface configuration:

```yang
module simple {
namespace "http://example.com/simple"; prefix simple;
container interfaces { list interface {
key "name"; leaf name {
type string;
}
leaf enabled { type boolean;
}
}
}
}
```

Parsing the YANG model:

Use the `yang` tools to generate Go code from your YANG model. This allows you to work with your data model in Go directly.

```bash
goyang -f go -o models models/simple.yang
```

Implementing the gNMI Client

Now that we have our YANG model ready, we can proceed

173

to implement the gNMI client. Below is a basic implementation to connect to a gNMI target:

Create a gNMI Client:

In your `client/client.go`, implement the client that communicates with the gNMI server.

```go
package client

import (

"context" "log"

"time"

"google.golang.org/grpc"

gnmi "github.com/openconfig/gnmi/proto/gnmi"

)

type GNMIClient struct { client gnmi.GNMIClient

}

func NewGNMIClient(target string) (*GNMIClient, error)
{ conn, err := grpc.Dial(target, grpc.WithInsecure())

if err != nil { return nil, err

}

return &GNMIClient{

client: gnmi.NewGNMIClient(conn),

}, nil

}

func (c *GNMIClient) SetInterface(name string, enabled
```

```go
bool) {

ctx, cancel := context.WithTimeout(context.Background(),
10*time.Second) defer cancel()

update := &gnmi.Update{

Path: []string{"interfaces", "interface", name},

Val:   &gnmi.TypedValue{Value:
&gnmi.TypedValue_JsonVal{JsonVal: []byte(enabled)}},

}

_, err := c.client.Set(ctx, &gnmi.SetRequest{Update:
[]*gnmi.Update{update}}) if err != nil {

log.Fatalf("Failed to set interface: %v", err)

}

log.Printf("Interface %s set to %t", name, enabled)

}
```

Using the Client in main.go:

Integrate the client into your `main.go` to perform configuration actions.

```go
package main

import (

"fmt"

"log"

"openconfig-demo/client"
```

175

```go
)
func main() {

target := "localhost:50051" // Replace with your gNMI server address gNMIClient, err := client.NewGNMIClient(target)

if err != nil {

log.Fatalf("Failed to create gNMI client: %v", err)

}

// Perform a set operation gNMIClient.SetInterface("eth0", true)


fmt.Println("Finished setting interface configuration.")

}
```
```

## Running the Implementation

With the setup complete, you can now run your application:

```bash
go run main.go
```

Make sure your gNMI target is reachable and that the necessary OpenConfig protocols are listening for incoming requests.

We covered setting up a basic Go environment, defining OpenConfig models in YANG, and implementing a gNMI client. This setup can serve as a foundation for building

176
```

more complex networking applications that interact with various devices in a centralized manner. As network environments continue to evolve, the use of OpenConfig alongside modern programming languages like Go will become increasingly important in the quest for automation, efficiency, and interoperability.

Chapter 10: Building a Testing Environment

A properly configured testing environment enables network engineers and operators to validate configurations, test changes, and troubleshoot issues without disrupting live network systems. This chapter will guide you through the steps necessary to build an effective and efficient testing environment for network automation.

10.1 Importance of a Testing Environment

Before delving into the specifics of building a testing environment, it's crucial to understand its significance. A testing environment serves several purposes:

Risk Mitigation: Changes in network configurations can lead to unintended outages or performance degradation. A testing environment allows for simulation and validation before going live.

Validation of Automation Scripts: As automation becomes more prevalent, the scripts used can introduce errors or create unexpected results. Testing before deployment ensures that the scripts work as intended.

Performance Benchmarking: A testing environment allows network engineers to measure the performance impact of new configurations or automation processes. This insight is vital for capacity planning and optimization.

Training and Development: New team members can use the testing environment to familiarize themselves with network configurations and automation tools without the fear of disrupting live services.

10.2 Components of a Testing Environment

To establish a functional testing environment in network automation, several essential components should be considered:

10.2.1 Virtualization

Virtualization technology enables the creation of virtual instances of network devices, eliminating the need for extensive physical hardware. Tools such as Cisco VIRL, GNS3, and EVE-NG allow engineers to design and simulate virtual networks that closely mirror production environments.

Benefits: Cost-effective, scalable, and allows for easy replication of network topologies.

Considerations: Ensure that the virtualization solution supports the specific devices and protocols prevalent in your network.

10.2.2 Configuration Management Tools

Configuration management tools such as Ansible, Puppet, or Chef can help automate the provisioning and configuration of devices within the testing environment. These tools enable teams to manage configurations consistently across multiple testing instances.

Benefits: Simplifies deployment, allows for repeatability, and can integrate with version control systems (like Git) for tracking changes.

10.2.3 Test Frameworks

Integrating a robust testing framework—such as Robot Framework, pytest, or NAPALM—enables the execution of predefined tests on your automation scripts and configurations. These frameworks can automate the testing process, ensuring that every change is thoroughly vetted before deployment.

Benefits: Reduces the time spent on manual testing and provides clear reports on the health and functionality of configurations.

10.2.4 Monitoring Tools

Monitoring tools are essential for evaluating the performance and reliability of automation in your testing environment. Tools such as Nagios, Zabbix, or Prometheus can provide insights into resource utilization and service health, ensuring that automated changes are yielding the desired results.

Benefits: Helps in identifying bottlenecks or performance issues before changes affect users. ## 10.3 Designing the Testing Environment

With the components identified, the next step is to design your testing environment. This involves several key considerations:

10.3.1 Topology Design

Design your network topology to closely resemble the production environment. This can include routers, switches, firewalls, and any other network components required for testing. Create multiple scenarios reflecting different aspects of network operations.

10.3.2 Environment Isolation

It's important to isolate the testing environment from the production network. This can be achieved through the use of virtual networks or dedicated VLANs to ensure that tests do not inadvertently affect live operations.

10.3.3 Resource Allocation

Consider the hardware and software resources required for your testing environment. Ensure that you have allocated enough CPU, memory, and storage to support the testing of complex configurations and automation scripts.

10.3.4 Backups and Snapshots

Implement a backup and snapshot strategy for your testing environment. This allows you to roll back changes easily if something goes wrong, providing an additional layer of safety during testing.

10.4 Best Practices for Testing

Building a testing environment requires careful planning and execution. Here are some best practices to follow:

Document Everything: Maintain clear documentation of your testing environment, including topology diagrams, configurations, and test cases. This aids in troubleshooting and knowledge transfer among team members.

Automate Where Possible: Utilize automation tools to streamline the setup and teardown of test environments. Automating repetitive tasks can save time and reduce human error.

Regularly Update the Environment: Ensure that your testing environment reflects the production environment's current state, including updates to systems and configurations. Regular updates prevent discrepancies and ensure valid testing results.

Involve Stakeholders: Engage relevant stakeholders in the design and testing process. Input from various perspectives can enhance the testing environment and ensure it meets the needs of the team.

By leveraging virtualization, configuration management tools, testing frameworks, and monitoring solutions, network professionals can create an environment that effectively supports automated processes while ensuring reliability and performance. As you proceed to implement your testing environment, remember the importance of documentation, automation, and stakeholder involvement to ensure success in your network automation journey.

Setting Up a Network Test Lab

Network testing is integral in today's software development landscape, particularly for applications that rely heavily on network communications. By creating a network test lab, developers can simulate different network conditions and monitor behaviors without the risk of disrupting live environments. By the end, you'll have a comprehensive understanding of the foundational components and practical examples to help you get started.

1. Introduction to Network Testing

Network testing involves validating the functionality, performance, and security of network components. In a dynamic environment, where microservices and continuous integration/continuous deployment (CI/CD) practices dominate, the need for a controlled environment to test network interactions becomes paramount. Using Go for this purpose can be beneficial due to its built-in concurrency, robust standard library, and cross-platform compatibility.

1.1 Goals of a Network Test Lab

When designing a network test lab, it's essential to have clear goals:

Simulate real-world scenarios: Create different network conditions such as latency, packet loss, and bandwidth constraints.

Isolate tests: Ensure that the tests do not impact live systems.

Automate testing: Use scripts to run tests efficiently and accurately. ## 2. Prerequisites and Setup

Before diving into the coding part, let's ensure you have the necessary prerequisites. ### 2.1 Install Go

If you haven't already installed Go, download and install the latest version from the [official Go website](https://golang.org/dl/). After installation, verify by running:

```bash
go version
```

2.2 Set Up Development Environment

Choose your favorite IDE or text editor for Go development. Popular choices include Visual Studio Code, GoLand, and Sublime Text. These editors typically offer great support for Go-specific features like syntax highlighting, auto-completion, and debugging.

2.3 Dependencies

For network simulation, we'll employ a few libraries. Here are some essential packages:

`github.com/julienschmidt/httprouter`: A lightweight router for building HTTP servers.

`github.com/stretchr/testify`: For writing assertions in tests.

`golang.org/x/net/nettest`: To help with testing network conditions. Use Go's package manager to install these dependencies:

```bash
go get github.com/julienschmidt/httprouter go get github.com/stretchr/testify

go get golang.org/x/net/nettest
```

3. Project Structure

Create a new directory for your project, and within it, establish a basic structure:

```
```

network-test-lab/ main.go

mocks/ mock_server.go

tests/

network_tests.go

``` ` ` ` ```

main.go: The entry point of your application.

mocks/: Contains implementations of mock servers for testing.

tests/: Directory for various test cases and scenarios.
4. Creating a Mock Server

In `mock_server.go`, create a simple HTTP server that can simulate response delays and different statuses:

```go
package mocks

import ( "fmt" "net/http" "time"
)

func StartMockServer(port string, delay time.Duration) {
http.HandleFunc("/", func(w  http.ResponseWriter,  r
*http.Request) {

time.Sleep(delay) w.WriteHeader(http.StatusOK)

fmt.Fprintf(w, "Response from mock server with %v delay", delay)
})

fmt.Printf("Mock       server       running       at
http://localhost:%s\n",       port)       if       err       :=
http.ListenAndServe(":"+port, nil); err != nil {
```
```

```go
        panic(err)
    }
}
```
```

This code sets up a simple HTTP server that introduces a configurable delay before responding, mimicking network latencies.

## 5. Writing Tests

In `network_tests.go`, we'll write tests that interact with our mock server:

```go
package tests
import ( "io/ioutil" "net/http" "testing" "time"
"network-test-lab/mocks"
)
func TestMockServerWithDelay(t *testing.T) {
go mocks.StartMockServer("8080", 2*time.Second)
time.Sleep(1 * time.Second) // Wait for the server to start
resp, err := http.Get("http://localhost:8080")
if err != nil {
t.Fatalf("Failed to connect to mock server: %v", err)
}
defer resp.Body.Close()
body, _ := ioutil.ReadAll(resp.Body) if resp.StatusCode !=
http.StatusOK {
```
```

```
    t.Errorf("Expected status OK; got %v", resp.Status)
}

expectedSubstring := "Response from mock server with" if
!strings.Contains(string(body), expectedSubstring) {
    t.Errorf("Expected response to contain %q; got %q",
expectedSubstring, string(body))
    }
}
```

This test starts the mock server in the background and sends an HTTP GET request. It then checks if the response is as expected.

6. Running the Tests

To run the tests, simply use:

```bash
go test ./tests
```

6.1 Simulating Different Scenarios

Expand your test cases by varying the delays, simulating packet loss, and introducing different HTTP status responses. This will bring diversity into your testing scenarios, mimicking real-world unpredictability.

Setting up a network test lab in Go fills a crucial gap in network testing practices. You can simulate various network conditions and scenarios while ensuring that your applications behave as expected under different circumstances. This chapter provided you with foundational tools and examples to get started, but the potential applications of this lab methodology are extensive.

Automating Network Tests with Go

The complexity of modern applications requires an equally sophisticated approach to network testing. This chapter focuses on how the Go programming language can be leveraged to automate network tests, streamlining workflows, and ensuring robust network performance.

Introduction to Network Testing

Network testing involves evaluating various aspects of a network, including its performance, reliability, security, and scalability. Key objectives of network testing include ensuring high availability, measuring response times, detecting bottlenecks, and verifying conformance to protocols. Historically, these tasks have been performed manually, which is not only time-consuming but also prone to human error.

Why Go for Network Testing?

Go, also known as Golang, is an open-source programming language developed by Google. Its features make it particularly well-suited for network programming and testing:

Concurrency: Go's goroutines provide efficient handling of multiple tasks simultaneously. This is essential for testing network performance under load or simulating various network scenarios.

Simplicity and Speed: Go is designed to be simple and efficient, allowing developers to write concise and readable code that compiles quickly, making it ideal for rapid prototyping and testing.

Standard Library: Go comes with an extensive standard library that includes powerful networking capabilities, making it easy to create, manage, and test network connections.

Cross-Platform Compatibility: Go applications can be built and run on various platforms, which helps in testing network configurations across different environments.

In this chapter, we will explore how to create automated network tests using Go, focusing on practical coding examples and best practices.

Setting Up the Environment

Before diving into coding, you need to set up your development environment. ### Installation

Go Installation: First, download and install Go from the official site [golang.org](https://golang.org/dl/). Follow the instructions based on your operating system.

Setup IDE: Choose an Integrated Development Environment (IDE) or text editor of your choice. Popular options include Visual Studio Code, Goland, and Atom with Go extensions.

Create a Workspace: Set up a directory for your Go projects. For instance, we can create a directory called `network-tests`.

```bash
mkdir ~/network-tests cd ~/network-tests
```

Initialize a Go Module: In your project directory, run the following command to create a new Go module.

```bash
go mod init network-tests
```

Writing Your First Network Test

Let's begin with a simple example: testing the reachability of a host. We will implement a function that checks if a given hostname is reachable and measure the response time.

Example: Ping Test

First, create a file called `ping_test.go`.

```go
package main

import (
"fmt"
"net"
"time"
)
// ping function to check connectivity
```

```go
func ping(host string) (time.Duration, error) { start :=
time.Now()

_, err := net.LookupHost(host) if err != nil {

return 0, err

}

return time.Since(start), nil

}

func main() {

host := "google.com" duration, err := ping(host) if err !=
nil {

fmt.Printf("Failed to ping %s: %v\n", host, err) return


}
```

```

}
fmt.Printf("Ping %s: %v\n", host, duration)
```

Explanation

Importing Packages: We import the `fmt`, `net`, and `time` packages. The `net` package enables network-related functionalities, while `time` helps us measure response time.

Ping Function: The `ping` function attempts to look up the host name. If the name resolution is successful, it returns the time taken; otherwise, it returns an error.

Main Function: In the `main` function, we specify the host we want to test, call the `ping` function, and print the results.

Running Your Test

To execute your test, run the following command in the terminal:

```bash
go run ping_test.go
```

You should see output indicating the response time for the specified host. ## Advanced Testing: Load Testing

To ensure that our network can handle the anticipated load, we can simulate multiple connections concurrently. Let's extend our example to perform a load test.

Example: Concurrent Ping Tests Create another file called `load_test.go`.

```go
package main
import (
"fmt"
"net"
"sync"
"time"
)
```

```go
// Ping function
func ping(host string) (time.Duration, error) { start :=
time.Now()
_, err := net.LookupHost(host) if err != nil {
return 0, err
}
return time.Since(start), nil
}
func main() {
var wg sync.WaitGroup var mu sync.Mutex host :=
"google.com"
results := make([]time.Duration, 0) concurrentRequests
:= 10
for i := 0; i < concurrentRequests; i++ { wg.Add(1)
go func() {
defer wg.Done() duration, err := ping(host)

mu.Lock()
if err == nil {
results = append(results, duration)
} else {
fmt.Printf("Error pinging %s: %v\n", host, err)
}
mu.Unlock()
```

```
}()
}
```

wg.Wait()

```
// Calculate average response time var totalDuration
time.Duration for _, d := range results {
totalDuration += d
```


```
}
```
` ` `

```
}
```

```
averageDuration          :=          totalDuration          /
time.Duration(len(results))
```

```
fmt.Printf("Average response time for %d ping(s) to %s:
%v\n", len(results), host, averageDuration)
```

Explanation

Concurrency: We use a `sync.WaitGroup` to wait for all goroutines to finish, allowing us to run multiple ping tests simultaneously.

Mutex: A `sync.Mutex` is employed to manage concurrent access to the shared slice `results`, ensuring thread-safe operations.

Average Calculation: After all pings, we calculate and print the average response time. ### Running the Load Test

Execute the load test with:

```bash
go run load_test.go
```

You will receive an average response time for the specified number of concurrent pings. ## Best Practices for Network Testing

Error Handling: Always handle errors gracefully. This ensures tests fail loudly and provide useful debugging information.

Logging: Employ logging to capture test outputs, response times, and errors for future analysis.

Configuration Management: Store test configurations (like hostnames, numbers of requests, and timeouts) in separate configuration files or environment variables to enhance maintainability.

Environment Isolation: When testing in production-like environments, ensure that tests do not disrupt actual user traffic.

Continuous Integration/Continuous Deployment (CI/CD): Integrate network tests into your CI/CD pipeline to automate tests on deployments, ensuring network stability with every code change.

Automating network tests using Go presents an efficient way to ensure that network systems are robust, reliable, and performant. By implementing basic and advanced testing techniques, developers can easily identify issues before they affect end-users. As the complexity of network architectures grows, so does the importance of testing — a necessity that can be effectively managed through automation with Go.

Conclusion

As we reach the conclusion of "Network Automation with Go," it's essential to reflect on the transformative potential that Go programming offers for network operations. Throughout this book, we have explored the intricate landscape of network automation, revealing how Go's simplicity, performance, and concurrency model make it an ideal choice for building scalable applications in the networking domain.

We have learned how to leverage Go's robust libraries and frameworks to automate tedious tasks that once consumed valuable time and resources. By integrating Go with network protocols and tools, you can create solutions that not only enhance productivity but also make networks more resilient and responsive. The practical examples and hands-on projects presented in this book provide a solid foundation for readers to apply these concepts in real-world scenarios.

As the landscape of network operations continues to evolve, embracing automation becomes increasingly critical. The skills and insights gained from this book empower you to harness the power of Go to streamline processes, reduce human error, and ultimately create a more efficient network environment. The applications you build will not only serve immediate needs but will also lay the groundwork for future developments, ensuring that your network operations remain agile in an ever-changing technology landscape.

In closing, we encourage you to take the knowledge from this book and experiment boldly. Push the boundaries of what you can achieve with network automation and Go. The future is bright for those who are willing to innovate and adapt, and we are excited to see the remarkable solutions you will create.

Thank you for joining us on this journey into the world of network automation. We hope this ebook has inspired you and provided you with the tools needed to advance your career in network operations with Go. Happy coding!

Biography

Tommy Clark is a passionate and dynamic author who combines a deep love for technology with an insatiable curiosity for innovation. As the mastermind behind the book *"Clark: A Journey Through Expertise and Innovation,"* Tommy brings years of hands-on experience in web development, web applications, and system administration to the forefront, offering readers a unique and insightful perspective.

With a strong background in Go programming and an ever-evolving fascination with crafting robust, efficient systems, Tommy excels at turning complex technical concepts into practical, actionable strategies. Whether building cutting-edge web solutions or diving into the intricate details of system optimization, Tommy's expertise is both broad and profound.

When not immersed in coding or writing, Tommy enjoys

exploring the latest tech trends, tinkering with open-source projects, and mentoring aspiring developers. His enthusiasm for technology and dedication to empowering others shine through in everything he creates.

Join Tommy Clark on this exciting journey to unlock the full potential of technology—and get ready to be inspired, informed, and equipped to tackle your next big challenge!

Glossary: Network Automation with Go

A

API (Application Programming Interface)

A set of rules and protocols that allows different software applications to communicate with each other. In network automation, APIs are often used to interact with network devices and services.

Automation

The use of technology to perform tasks without human intervention. In the context of network automation, it refers to the process of configuring, managing, and monitoring network devices through scripts and automation tools.

B

Bash

A Unix shell and command language that is commonly used for scripting. While Go is often preferred for its performance and type safety, Bash scripts are still widely used in automation tasks.

C

CLI (Command Line Interface)

A text-based interface used to interact with computer systems and software. Network engineers often use CLI to configure devices manually, but automation tools can replace some of these tasks for efficiency.

Configuration Management

The process of systematically handling changes to ensure that a network's performance and security parameters are maintained. Tools that support configuration management help automate deployment, updates, and compliance checks.

D

Device

In networking, a device refers to any physical hardware component connected to a network (e.g., routers, switches, firewalls) that can be configured or monitored.

Desired State Configuration

An approach that defines the desired state of network devices and ensures that they remain in that state. Automation tools use this model to apply changes, roll back configurations, or report deviations.

E

ETL (Extract, Transform, Load)

A data processing framework often used in network analytics. In the context of network automation, ETL can be applied to gather device data, transform it into a usable format, and load it into analytics tools.

G

Go (Golang)

An open-source programming language developed by Google. Known for its efficiency and concurrency, Go is increasingly being adopted for network automation due to its strong standard library, Go modules, and ease of use.

Goroutine

A lightweight thread managed by the Go runtime. Goroutines are used to execute functions concurrently, making Go particularly suited for automating tasks that involve multiple network devices simultaneously.

H

HashiCorp Terraform

An open-source infrastructure-as-code software tool that enables users to define and provision data center infrastructure through a high-level configuration language. Terraform can be integrated with Go to automate network infrastructures.

I

Infrastructure as Code (IaC)

The practice of managing and provisioning computing infrastructure through machine-readable configuration files rather than physical hardware configuration or interactive configuration tools.

Intent-Based Networking (IBN)

A networking approach that uses high-level policies to automatically configure and manage underlying network infrastructure. It focuses on the desired outcome rather than the means to achieve it, making network automation more intuitive.

J

JSON (JavaScript Object Notation)

A lightweight data interchange format that is easy to read and write for humans and machines. JSON is widely used in network automation for data serialized formats, especially when working with APIs.

L

Library

A collection of pre-written code that users can incorporate into their own programs. In Go, libraries are used to simplify tasks related to network automation, such as interacting with device APIs or parsing configurations.

N

Network Topology

The arrangement of different elements (links, nodes, etc.) in a computer network. Understanding network topology is crucial for automation tasks, as it influences how devices and their configurations are managed.

NetConf

A network management protocol developed by the IETF that uses XML to provide a mechanism for installing, manipulating, and deleting the configuration of network devices.

P

Playbook

In the context of network automation, a playbook is a collection of automation tasks defined in a specific format. Tools like Ansible use YAML to structure playbooks, while Go-based automation systems may implement their own definitions.

Python

A high-level programming language often used for network automation. While Go is gaining traction for its performance advantages, many existing network automation tools leverage Python's simplicity and rich ecosystem.

R

REST (Representational State Transfer)

An architectural style that defines a set of constraints used for creating Web Services. RESTful APIs provide a standard way for tools and scripts to interact with network devices.

S

SNMP (Simple Network Management Protocol)

A standard protocol used for managing and monitoring network devices. Network automation scripts often use SNMP for gathering statistics and monitoring performance.

Script

A program or sequence of instructions that is executed by a computer. Scripts automate repetitive tasks without the need for human intervention and can be written in various programming languages, including Go.

T

Template

A pre-designed format that can be filled with data to generate configurations or documents. In network automation, templates are often used to standardize device configuration files across multiple devices.

Telemetry

The collection of measurements and monitoring data from network devices. Telemetry provides real-time insights into the performance and health of network infrastructure.

U

UDP (User Datagram Protocol)

A communication protocol used across the internet for time-sensitive transmissions such as video streaming or online gaming, where speed is essential, and error recovery is less critical.

V

Version Control

A system that records changes to a file or set of files over time. In network automation, version control is crucial for tracking changes in configurations and scripts, ensuring accountability and facilitating collaboration.

Y

YAML (YAML Ain't Markup Language)

A human-readable data serialization standard that is often used for configuration files. Many network automation tools, including Ansible and SaltStack, utilize YAML for defining playbooks and settings.

www.ingramcontent.com/pod-product-compliance
Lightning Source LLC
LaVergne TN
LVHW051329050326
832903LV00031B/3435